THE SEVENTH REGIMENT: A RECORD

BY
MAJOR GEORGE L. WOOD

AUTHOR'S PREFACE.

The following pages were written for the purpose of making a permanent record of the facts within the author's knowledge relating to the Seventh Ohio Regiment. The work was undertaken with the belief that the doings and sufferings of the regiment were of sufficient magnitude and importance to entitle it to a separate record. It has been extremely difficult to obtain facts, on account of so large a portion of the members still being in the service. The book is, therefore, written principally from memory. If it serves to perpetuate in the minds of the public the hardships, as well as long and faithful service, of this gallant regiment, then the object of the author is accomplished.

Warren, *May, 1865.*

PREFACE.

This preface to the history of the Seventh Ohio Volunteer Infantry is written at the request of the accomplished author of the book; but without having read it, seen it, or heard its contents. I have, however, such confidence in the ability, honesty, candor, good judgment, and good taste of my old friend and "companion in arms," that, for myself, I take his work on trust, and in cheerful faith commend it to others.

But was there a demand for another book on the war? Or were the doings and sufferings of one regiment, among the thousands engaged in the war, of such interest as to demand a separate history? These are questions the author doubtless weighed carefully before he began to write; and his answer to them is his book. I agree with him. This nation has a deep, and will have a lasting, interest in the war. We have been making history of unrivalled, perhaps of unequalled, importance to the world during the past four years. We ourselves cannot comprehend the magnitude of the work we have been doing, or, rather, that God has been doing through us. The successful revolts of the Netherlanders against the tyranny of Philip II.—of the Puritans against the tyranny of Charles I.—of the republicans against the tyranny of George III., dwindle to insignificance (important as they were) in comparison with the successful revolt of the loyal, Union-loving, freedom-loving citizens of this Republic against the tyranny of treason and slavery. It was a great fight for a great cause, and God has given us a great victory. There was not a nation on earth that was not interested in the conflict. Ay, it concerned our common humanity. All this will be seen more clearly and felt more deeply twenty, fifty, a hundred years hence than now. But to transmit and perpetuate the fruits of this victory we must have records of the war—many records, made from many different points of view, and of many kinds, great and small. The history of this war is not yet written, perhaps cannot be successfully written for many years yet. And that it may one day be written as it should be, every regiment that has a story to tell should tell it. These regimental histories will be invaluable to the Bancroft who, fifty years hence, shall write the history of this war. The world is only beginning to understand the true character and vocation of history—*to make the past live in the present*; not in great pageants, not in processions of kings, princes, and mighty conquerors, but *in the common every-day speech and deeds of the people*. When Merle d'Aubigné would write the History of the Reformation, he wrote to Guizot for counsel. Guizot encouraged him, and counselled him to proceed, but added, "*Give us facts, incidents, details.*" This counsel chimed with the purpose and genius of d'Aubigné, and the result was a history that, though it discusses doctrines and themes commonly held to be dry and uninteresting, has for old and young, and men of all classes, all the charm of romance. In this, his "facts, incidents, details," equally with his fascinating style, lies the charm of the histories of Macaulay. But that historians may write such histories—that the historian of this war may write such a history, the "facts, incidents, details" must be on record. There is a demand, therefore, for another book, for many other books, on the war.

In addition to this, every regiment of the grand Army of the Union in this war has its own history, of peculiar interest to its own especial friends. And I have faith in what Dr. O. W. Holmes once said: "I would not give a fig for a man every one of whose geese were not better than any other man's swans." To us of the old Seventh "all our geese were swans." Whether others believed in us or not, we had faith in ourselves and in one another; we were a mutual admiration society of a thousand and odd men. And the fact is, that, for some reason, but what I cannot say, the Seventh Regiment, from the day it was mustered into service to the day it was mustered out, was always the pride and pet of Ohio, of Northern Ohio especially. In this respect it never had a rival. True, it was a well-disciplined, gallant, fighting regiment; but so were many others. True, it had brave and accomplished officers; but so had many others. True, it had in the ranks men of refinement, education, and high social position; but so had many others. I am at a loss to account for it, but the fact nevertheless was as I have stated it; and as its deeds corresponded with its renown, *its* doings, of all others, demand a permanent record. And, if I am not mistaken, the reader of the following pages who shall follow the Seventh from the day it was mustered into service, in Cleveland, in 1861, to the day the pitiful remnant of it, after tramping and fighting over almost half the Union, were mustered out of service, in Cleveland, in 1864, will find in them ample compensation for his time.

F. T. B.

Chicago, Ill., *May, 1865*.

CHAPTER I.

The fall of Sumter.—Civil war begun.—Preparations by the South.—Nobility.

On a gloomy day in April, 1861, the telegraph flashed the news over the country that Fort Sumter, a fortress belonging to the United States, had been fired upon by a body of rebels, and thus inaugurating all the horrors of civil war.

By the great mass of people, civil war in our hitherto peaceful country was entirely unlooked for. It burst so suddenly, that the entire country was convulsed.

The people had become so accustomed to clamor in Congress and elsewhere, that they looked upon these threats to dissolve the Union as mere bravado.

After the first clash of arms at Fort Sumter, both North and South drew back in alarm, as if in fear of the coming storm. The Southern people, however, better prepared by education for scenes of strife and bloodshed, received the news of the inauguration of civil war with less alarm than did those of the North. The latter received it with a fearful dignity, conscious of the power to crush the rebellion. The South, with that arrogance that becomes her so well, expected to make an easy conquest. Long-continued exercise of power in national matters, had taught her to look upon the people of the Free States as her inferiors, needing but a master-stroke for their subjugation,—willing to lay down their arms, and seek safety in dishonor. They had taken us for a race of cowards, because we had given way to their selfish demands in our public councils, for the sake of peace. To be sure, we had some daring spirits in Congress who met these bullying traitors, making them feel the full force of Northern valor. But these were isolated cases, and won the respect of the Southern people to the persons of the actors rather than to the North as a people. They looked upon these spirited examples as rather proving the fact of our want of chivalry than otherwise, and therefore were not corrected in their false estimate of a people whom they were about to meet on bloody fields.

One reason the South had for cherishing so mean an opinion of the North as a military power, was on account of her having entirely neglected the cultivation of the art of war. She had so few representatives in the army and navy, that they were both almost entirely within the control of the South.

This control the latter had exercised for years, until her people came to look upon themselves as the only persons in the country fit to bear arms. They flattered themselves that they were the army, and we but a rabble, to be dispersed beyond the hope of reorganization at the first clash of arms. But in this strife, like all others where aristocratic privilege comes in contact with the freedom of democracy, these arrogant lords were to meet with a bitter disappointment; they were to be made to respect the strong muscle and brave hearts of the so-styled plebeian North.

This avowed hostility of the South to the North had caused the former to take a military direction, and forced her into a course of policy which, however outrageous it might appear, was yet a matter of necessity in her attempt at independence. The first step was to put herself upon a war-footing. This she had been perfecting for several years. The next was to get the Government so in her control as to make it powerless in the incipient stages of the rebellion, that it might gain sufficient strength to withstand the first shock, and thus gain precedence.

During a period of thirty years the South was gradually assuming a war-footing. The militia was organized; independent companies were formed with no warlike object, as was generally supposed, but really to resist any encroachment of the Federal Government upon what the leaders deemed the rights of the Southern people. The election of Abraham Lincoln to the presidency was not the cause of civil war, but only its apology. There had existed in the minds of the Southern people a desire for an independent government, which would give the aristocracy a firmer footing. In other words, the Federal Government was too democratic. But it was necessary that these conspirators have some apparently good reason for civil war; else the people who were at heart right, would desert them at a time when they were most needed. The time for the inauguration of civil war was therefore most fitly chosen. The people were made to believe that the inauguration of President Lincoln was a sufficient reason; and thus the dream of thirty years of these disunionists was at last realized. The apology for the war had been substituted for its cause, and the mass of the Southern people made eager to meet those on bloody fields whom they were led to suppose were about to deprive them of their rights and precipitate them into ruin.

There is always a class styled the nobility in every nation. But the true nobility in America is that class who have won that distinction by noble deeds; who are great, not in titles and garters of nobility, but in great achievements: not that class who base their right to that title upon the number and character of human beings they may own. The American people hold that distinction must be given to those by whom it is merited; and that it cannot be the subject of monopoly. Each person, however mean his birth, has the same right to enter the list for the prize as he who was born of a higher rank. It is this freedom, which is given to all, that has caused the Northern States to make such rapid progress towards civilization and greatness; and it is the crippling of this great principle that has cast a shadow over the enslaved South. One great object of the leaders of the South had been to arrest the rapid growth of the North, which, they were conscious, would one day throw them into a helpless minority, for they could not themselves keep pace with this rapid progress. Their ambition was to have capital control labor, while the laboring classes were to be subservient to the capitalists, and a sort of serfdom forced upon them. The wealthy class were to live in luxury and indolence upon the unrequited toil of their slaves. These facts, the leaders of the wicked rebellion, which they were to inaugurate, were careful to conceal from their followers. This was so well done, that the people of the South thought that these imaginary wrongs of the Government, which had been pictured to them by their masters, was the true reason of their attempt at separation from the Union. It is hoped that the masses will soon see the difference between serving a privileged class of aristocrats, and being members of a free Republic.

CHAPTER II.

The President's call for troops.—Organization of the Seventh.—Its departure for Camp Dennison.—Its reorganization and departure for the field.

On Monday, April 15, the President issued a call for 75,000 volunteers for three months' service. The States responded immediately to this call in double the number required. Never in the history of the world was such a response witnessed to the call of any country. Men left their implements of husbandry in the fields and rushed to the recruiting stations. The executives of the States were pressed with applications to raise companies and batteries under the call of the President.

Under this call thirteen regiments of infantry were assigned to Ohio. In fifteen days 71,000 troops were offered to Governor Dennison to fill the quota of the State. Camps were now established at different points in the State, and troops ordered to rendezvous. Camp Taylor, at Cleveland, Ohio, was organized on the 22d day of April, and by the 27th contained several thousand troops. Of these, the city of Cleveland had three companies of infantry; Trumbull County, one; Mahoning County, one company of infantry and a section of artillery; Portage County, two; Lake County, one; Lorain County, one; Huron County, one; while the city of Toledo was represented by an entire regiment. The latter part of April these detached companies were formed into a regiment, constituting the Seventh Ohio. It contained the right material for a fighting regiment. The majority of its members were of a floating class, fond of adventure, while many were of the best class. The regiment, as a whole, combined rare military talent. Many of its officers and privates were skilled in tactics; and those who were not, immediately set themselves about acquiring the necessary information, rather by practice than study; for, with some exceptions, it was not a scholarly regiment. The members took too much the character of adventurers, to indulge in close study or profound thinking. But for practical purposes, I doubt whether the regiment had a superior in the State. It readily acquired discipline while on duty; but while off duty, its members were not over-nice in their conduct, seldom indulging in sports that were absolutely wrong, but, at the same time, gratifying that propensity for fun which characterized them through their entire career. It contained no drones; there was no companionship in it for such.

On a beautiful Sabbath in early May, as the morning, with its freshness, was dispelling the damps and shadows of the night from city and country, a regiment was seen passing down the streets of the city of Cleveland. The sweet strains of music and the heavy tramp of the soldiers alone broke the silence. There was nothing but this martial bearing, which marked the carriage of the members of the regiment, to distinguish them from the multitude which was hastening in the same direction; for there were no arms and no uniforms. Each member was dressed in his citizen's garb, and there was no attempt at military evolutions. It was a simple march of determined men to the defence of their country. Solemnity and a becoming absence of unnecessary enthusiasm marked the occasion with sublimity and grandeur. The faces of those brave men were saddened with the thought of the perils which lay before them, and the endearments that were behind. They were marching to perform a sacred trust, confided to them by their countrymen. "This was the first march of the gallant Seventh." Arriving at the depot of the Cleveland, Columbus, and Cincinnati Railroad, it took a train of cars for Camp Dennison, where it arrived in the afternoon of the next day. Here they were totally unprepared to receive it, no barracks having been erected, although one hundred men had been sent there for that purpose several days previous. The ground was perfectly saturated with water from a three days' rain, and the camp in what had been a cornfield. But notwithstanding these difficulties, by sunset the regiment had constructed barracks, and were comparatively comfortable. In a few days the companies began to drill in earnest, and their advancement was correspondingly rapid.

On the 11th day of May the regiment was ordered to elect, by ballot, three field-officers. The candidates for colonel were, E. B. Tyler, of Ravenna; a former brigadier of militia, and James A. Garfield. The former was elected. Garfield afterwards became colonel of the Forty-second regiment, and, in command of a brigade, defeated Humphrey Marshall in Kentucky, for which he was given a star. Captain W. R. Creighton was elected lieutenant-colonel, and J. S. Casement, of Painesville, major.

On the 13th day of May, the President having issued a call for 42,032 volunteers for three years, a meeting was held in the Seventh Regiment, when all but one of the officers were in favor of organizing under this call. The subject being brought before the regiment on the following day, about three-fourths of the command enlisted for the three years' service. Recruiting officers were sent home, and by the middle of June the regiment was full. It was mustered into the three years' service on the 19th and 20th of June.

The companies were officered as follows: Company A, O. J. Crane, captain; A. C. Burgess, first-lieutenant; D. A. Kimball, second-lieutenant. Company B, James T. Sterling, captain; Joseph B. Molyneaux, first-lieutenant; H. Z. Eaton, second-lieutenant. Company C, Giles W. Shurtliff, captain; Judson N. Cross, first-lieutenant; E. Hudson Baker, second-lieutenant. Company D, John N. Dyer, captain; Charles A. Weed, first-lieutenant; A. J. Williams, second-lieutenant. Company E, John W. Sprague, captain; Arthur T. Wilcox, first-lieutenant; Ralph Lockwood, second-lieutenant. Company F, D. B. Clayton, captain; John B. Rouse, first-lieutenant; A. C. Day, second-lieutenant. Company G, F. A. Seymour, captain; W. H. Robinson, first-lieutenant; E. S. Quay, second-lieutenant. Company H, Joel F. Asper, captain; Geo. L. Wood, first-lieutenant; Halbert B. Case, second-lieutenant. Company I, W. R. Sterling, captain; Samuel McClelland, first-lieutenant; E. F. Fitch, second-lieutenant. Company K, John F. Schutte, captain; Oscar W. Sterl, first-lieutenant; C. A. Nitchelm, second-lieutenant. H. K. Cushing was appointed surgeon, and F. Salter assistant surgeon. John Morris was appointed quartermaster, Louis G. De Forest, adjutant, and Rev. F. T. Brown, chaplain.

Camp Dennison was well calculated for a camp of instruction. It is separated into two parts by the track of the Little Miami Railroad, while the river of the same name flows along its border. It is situated between sloping hills of some magnitude, in a slightly undulating valley. In summer it is beautiful; in winter, gloomy.

Soon after being mustered into service, the regiment was reviewed by George B. McClellan, then major-general of Ohio militia, commanding the Department of the Ohio. Immediately after, we were ordered to join his forces in the field.

Accordingly, on the afternoon of the 26th of June, the regiment took the cars for Columbus, Ohio, under command of Lieutenant-Colonel Creighton, Colonel Tyler having gone in advance. Arriving in Columbus late at night, it was transferred to the Central Ohio Railroad, arriving at Bell air in the afternoon of the succeeding day. It was immediately ordered across the river to Benwood, a small station on the Baltimore and Ohio Railroad, a few miles below Wheeling. Here the regiment was, for the first time, supplied with ammunition. It encamped on the common, after the pieces were loaded. Much fatigued by their long ride, the men threw themselves upon the hard ground, and were soon enjoying a sound sleep.

In the mean time Major Casement was superintending the transportation of the baggage and supplies across the river to a train of cars in waiting.

Here and there the dusky forms of men were seen grouped over the fires, which were dimly burning, discussing the stories which were floating about camp, with no apparent starting place, of ambuscades, masked batteries, and other concealed horrors.

Early on the morning of the 28th of June, three trains of cars were slowly conveying the regiment into the wilds of Western Virginia, where war, in its madness, was to confront it.

It arrived at Grafton early in the afternoon, and taking the Parkersburg branch of the railroad, it arrived at Clarksburg before the close of the day, and encamped in the outskirts of the village. The entire regiment occupied tents, which were looked upon with much more favor than densely crowded barracks.

While encamped at this place, a stand of colors was presented to the regiment, the gift of the Turners, a society of Germans in Cleveland.

Near thirty miles from the village of Clarksburg is the small hamlet of Weston, then a notorious haunt for rebels. In the place was a bank, in which the deposits, to the amount of about thirty thousand dollars, still remained. The authorities were desirous of procuring this treasure. The undertaking was intrusted to the Seventh. It was proposed to surprise the town early in the morning, before any one was astir to give the alarm.

In the afternoon of the last day of June, the regiment wound its way through the village, across the river, on to what is called the Clarksburg pike, leading to Weston. The clay was intensely hot, and the men entirely unused to marching. At sunset but little distance had been made, and all were much fatigued, but still the gallant band pressed onward. Weary and footsore, it moved on till daylight, when some considerable distance intervened between it and the village. Men were beginning to fall out by the wayside, unable to proceed further. At this unfortunate moment the river appeared in view, which makes a bend to the road, about a mile from Weston. On the opposite side of the road was a gradual slope of cultivated land, with here and there a clump of trees. From behind one of these a man was seen to emerge, and being taken for one of the enemy's scouts, the command was given to "fire," when several pieces were discharged, without injury, however, to the object of their aim. A double-quick was now ordered, when the men, unable to proceed with their knapsacks, scattered them along the road.

Arriving at the town the right wing made a detour to the left, while the left wing made a similar one to right, deploying as they went. In this manner the village was entirely surrounded. The first intimation the citizens had of the presence of the military was the playing of the "Star Spangled Banner" by the band stationed in the park. A guard was placed over the bank, and a member of the regiment detailed to look to the business.

The Union citizens were overjoyed at the presence of the Federal forces. They prepared a breakfast for the entire regiment, and other charitable acts, which attested their devotion to the Union cause. The regiment encamped on the bank of the river, near the cemetery.

During the first days of our stay at Weston many arrests were made of disloyal citizens, a few of whom were sent to Columbus, Ohio, to await the action of the Federal Government.

At this time a small force, under command of Lieutenant-Colonel Pond, of the Seventeenth Ohio Volunteers, was besieged at Glenville, a small village on the banks of the Little Kanawha, by a superior force of rebels, under command of Major Patton, assisted by Captain O. Jennings Wise. Companies H and B were sent to his relief. After a fatiguing march of two days and one night they opened communication with Colonel Pond, the rebels withdrawing at their approach.

Six more companies of the regiment arrived at Glenville on the following day, Colonel Tyler being fearful that the first detachment might meet with a reverse. Several other regiments arrived about the same time, but left soon after.

During the stay of the regiment at this place, many scouting expeditions were sent out; on which occasions many dangers and hardships were encountered.

Just before our arrival at Glenville, a Union lady rode in the saddle through the rebel camp, with the stars and stripes in one hand and a pistol in the other, while she defied the rebel host. Being pursued, she sought refuge in our camp, and finally accompanied the advance of our forces to her home, with the proud satisfaction of seeing the old banner once more planted on her native soil. During the progress of the war she had suffered many perils. At one time she went to visit her brother, who was concealed in the woods, for the purpose of giving him food, when she was challenged by a rebel picket. She wheeled her horse, and, by hard riding, escaped, the rebel bullets passing harmlessly over her head.

Private Adams, of Company C, was wounded while on picket, being the first casualty in the regiment produced by the enemy. About the same time Captain Shurtliff had a horse shot from under him, while riding in the vicinity of the camp, and within the Federal lines.

Some difficulty was experienced at this place in procuring supplies. The regiment was fed for some time on corn meal and fresh beef. A mill, however, was soon set in operation, and supplies of flour and meal were furnished in abundance.

CHAPTER III.

The pursuit of General Wise.—Tyler ordered to menace Gauley Bridge and threaten Wise's communications.

On the 11th day of July General Rosecrans, by order of General McClellan, marched his brigade eight miles through a mountain-path to the rear of the rebel force, occupying the crest of Rich Mountain, commanded by Colonel Pegram. This movement resulted in the fighting of the battle of that name. The rebels were completely defeated, and made a precipitate retreat towards Carrick's Ford, where, on the 13th, they were again routed, with the loss of their general.

In the mean time the rebel General Wise had occupied the Kanawha Valley, with a few regular troops and a considerable force of militia.

The advance of this force extended as far down the river as Buffalo, while numerous incursions were made by the rebel cavalry in the vicinity of Point Pleasant, a village situated at the junction of the Kanawha with the Ohio River.

To oppose this force General Cox was sent with a brigade of Ohio troops. His main force passed up the river in boats, while a sufficient force was kept on each flank to prevent surprise.

General Wise gradually retired at the advance of this force until, arriving on the banks of Scarey Creek, he threw up some breastworks, and awaited the approach of the Union troops.

While these movements were being executed in the valley, Colonel Tyler was ordered to advance with a brigade by the way of Sutton, to menace Gauley Bridge, and threaten Wise's communications.

On the 22d of July the Seventh Regiment moved out of Glenville, on what is called the Braxton road, towards Bulltown, where it was to be joined by Colonel Tyler with the Seventeenth Ohio, two companies of the First Virginia, with Captain Mack's battery, United States Artillery, and Captain Snyder's section of twelve-pounders, making a force of fifteen hundred.

We arrived at Bulltown in the evening of the next day, meeting with no resistance from the rebels, who were scattered in small parties through this entire region of country. We had expected to meet with opposition at the ford, on the Little Kanawha, some twenty miles from Glenville, but with the exception of a small band of guerilars, who were very careful to keep the river between ourselves and them, we saw no rebels.

It was not until the evening of the 25th that we broke camp, and then to cross a range of hills only, into the valley of the Elk, where we remained until the 27th of July.

At this camp we learned of a rebel force at Flat Woods, distant six miles, in the direction of Sutton. On the 27th we moved out, in a heavy rain, to attack their camp, but at our approach they fled in dismay.

We remained at Flat Woods till the following Sunday, when we moved on to Sutton, a distance of ten miles.

Sutton, the county-seat of Braxton County, is situated at the base of a high range of hills, on the right bank of the Elk River. The river is crossed by a suspension bridge. Back of the village, and about two hundred feet above it, is a fine table land, with a range of hills for a back ground. This table land was to be approached only by a narrow defile fronting the river, which was easily defended; for a battery properly planted would command every approach for a mile around; besides, the enemy would have to cross the Elk River under fire. Nature had made the position a strong one.

The command, now swelled to about two thousand, encamped on this table land, with the two companies of the First Virginia, and Mack's Battery thrown forward across the river, to keep open the road in front.

The command at once proceeded to erect fortifications, Captain Asper being sent to the front of Captain Mack's position on the Summerville pike, with instructions to select a proper position, after which to erect a fortification commanding the road. Finding a point where the road makes a sharp angle, the captain constructed the work, which, although of no account during the stay of the regiment at Sutton, afterwards proved a good point of defence, when the wreak garrison stationed there was attacked.

The second day of August, the regiment left Sutton, and crossing the river again advanced towards Gauley Bridge. The day was one of the hottest, which, added to the hilly nature of the country, made the advance difficult. Both officers and men fell out of the line, unable to proceed, being so oppressed by the heat, and wearied by the difficult state of the roads. At night we had crossed but one range of hills, and found ourselves in the valley of the Little Birch River, at the foot of Birch Mountain. The following morning we again took up the line of march, reaching the Great Birch River at early twilight, having made but a few miles during the day.

In the afternoon we were joined by our chaplain, who, when we were at Glenville, volunteered to make his way across the country with a message to General Cox. And now, after an absence of more than two weeks, on a perilous message, he was again with us, as fresh and light-hearted as when he left for his daring enterprise. He joined us by the way of Gauley Bridge, having been the first to make the trip. Alone, through a country infested by murderous bands of guerrillas and outlaws, he traveled more than a hundred and fifty miles. Before such deeds of individual heroism, all but the grandeur and magnitude of large battles fade into obscurity. In such single exploits there is a stern, silent daring, that obscures the maddened bravery of a battle-field.

From our chaplain we learned that General Wise had left the valley, burning the bridge over the Gauley River, after crossing his command. He had become frightened and fled. And thus the rebel general, who at Charleston had said: "By G—, the stars and stripes shall never wave over this town again;" on the Wednesday following exclaimed: "The enemy are on us, why the h—ll don't you pack my wagon," and, taking counsel of his fears, fled in dismay.

But let us return to the Seventh Regiment, which we left at its camp near the Big Birch River.

On the morning of August 6, we broke camp, and taking a mountain road arrived at Summerville on the following Wednesday, and encamped on Addison Hill.

The country about Summerville is beautiful in the extreme. It is slightly undulating, having more the appearance of an open country, or in some respects a prairie, than of a valley between two very high ridges. It is sufficiently rolling to hide the mountains which separate the Gauley from the Elk River.

At our former camp we were surrounded by very high, precipitous mountains, with large rocks projecting from their summits. After passing over Powell Mountain, we came into the valley of the Gauley, and after marching a short distance, entirely lost sight of these mountains, over whose rocky crests we had, but a short time before, pursued our slow and weary way.

The contrast between this camp and the one at Big Birch was striking. Here we were reminded of Ohio, our native State, the one which had more attractions for us than any other; while at the latter camp we were constantly reminded of some lonely country, described only by the novelist, and inhabited alone by robbers and outlaws. And yet, upon this mountain region, nature was lavish with her charms. The scenery is grand beyond description. Peak after peak rises, one above another, until the tired eye arrows dim in its endeavor to trace the outlines of the distant mountain, and seeks the beautiful valley, wherein to restore its lost vision.

From the top of Powell's Mountain, the beauty of the scenery is lost sight of in its magnificence. This mountain is the highest in Western Virginia, and commands the finest view. The first time I ascended it was on horseback. When near the top we struck into a bridle path, and, urging our horses into a gallop, we were soon at the base of the projecting rocks. Below, a lovely panorama was open to our view. The side of the mountain, as well as the distant valley, seemed covered with a carpet of green, for both were densely wooded, and in the distance the foliage seemed to blend with the earth. We could see far away into the smaller valleys, and from them trace the ravines, in which the small rivulets make their merry descent from the side of the mountain.

At last, tired of gazing at this beautiful spot in nature's varied scenery, we again urged our horses forward, and, after partially winding around the mountain, we were at the very summit of this mass of earth, rocks, and herbage. We now obtained a view of the opposite side of the mountain from which we had ascended, where beauty expands into sublimity. We could plainly trace the course of the Kanawha River, as on its banks the mountains rise higher, and are more abrupt, while beyond they lessen into hills, and the hills waste into a valley. On the side of the distant hills we could see an occasional farm, with its fields of golden grain ready for the harvest. On the very top of this mountain was living a family.

Notwithstanding their great height, these mountains seemed fertile; and the farms are apparently as good as those in the valley. Springs frequently make their way out of the rocks by the roadside. Water is abundant in any part of these mountains, and springs more common than in the valley.

Near the top of Powell's Mountain, in a kind of basin, is a very fine farm. It is well watered, and well timbered, and quite fertile. The owner lives and flourishes in this quiet home, and, I should say, is quite as happy as if in a city. He has become accustomed to the loneliness of his mountain retreat. The wild scenery has become familiar—its very wildness has a charm. He is content with two visits each year to the distant settlement. It is literally true that "home is where the heart is."

Although this country was well supplied with provisions of every kind, we were not allowed to appropriate any of it. The property of rebels was considered sacred. The authorities were confident of putting down the rebellion through clemency, and, therefore, were both ready and willing to put our soldiers upon half rations, rather than incur the ill-will of traitors. When prisoners were captured, they had what was called an oath of allegiance administered to them, when they were liberated, to again rob and plunder. Occasionally we captured a horse, but it was invariably given up, on the owner taking this oath of allegiance. In view of this moderate method of dealing with them, they risked nothing in prowling about our lines, for they knew that they had only to take this oath to procure an honorable discharge; while the soldiers of the Federal army, if they stole but an onion to make a piece of hard bread palatable, were subjected to the severest punishments. Experience has finally taught us, that hard blows alone will conquer a rebellion, and that to reduce a foe, starvation is quite as good as the bayonet.

I do not know that any one was criminal in this early practice of clemency towards rebels; it seemed rather to be a sort of national weakness, growing out of the universal opinion that the rebellion was, at the greatest, but a weak effort of a deluded people; and that kindness, connected with a show of strength, rather than its exercise, would induce them to return to their former allegiance. It seems to be, at this day, of little consequence why this practice prevailed, or who was responsible for it, as it has almost entirely ceased.

On the 11th day of August, Captain John W. Sprague was given a leave of absence, to go to his home, and was intrusted with dispatches to General Rosecrans. He was to proceed by the way of Sutton and Clarksburg. When near the Big Birch River he was suddenly confronted by a band of rebel cavalry, belonging to Colonel Croghan's Second Georgia Regiment, who was not far from the spot, with his entire command. The mail carrier and two dragoons, who accompanied Captain Sprague, attempted to make their escape; only one, however, was successful; the mail carrier receiving a mortal wound in the attempt.

Securing their prisoners, the rebel cavalry crossed the Gauley River, and were soon out of reach of the Federal forces. An unsuccessful attempt was made to rescue the captors; but infantry, of course, could make but a fruitless attempt at recapturing prisoners in the hands of well-mounted cavalry.

This occurrence spread a gloom over the entire camp. One of the best officers of the regiment had been captured almost within our lines, and borne away to a Southern prison, to endure the privations of prison life, with the fond anticipation of seeing home and friends blighted and withered. To be lost to one's country, within the prison walls of her enemies, when the arm of every true patriot is needed in her defence, is a sad fate.

I am not inclined to blame any one for this unfortunate occurrence, though it may occur to the mind of the reader that good generalship would require that the commandant of a body of troops, in the heart of an enemy's country, should know whether or not the cavalry of that enemy was hanging on his flank and rear. And then, again, it may be urged with truth that the command was almost entirely without cavalry, though it was furnished with one company, as well as one of Snake Hunters, as they were called. The legitimate business in the army of the latter was scouting. They had no other duty to perform.

But however these facts may be, yet true it is that a regiment of the enemy's regular cavalry was not only hanging on the flank of our column, but occupied our rear—thus severing our communications, and cutting off our supplies.

On the 15th day of August we again moved forward, after first sending a company down to Hugh's Ferry. We proceeded through a densely wooded country, abounding in laurel and pau-pau, arriving at Cross Lanes, two and a half miles from Carnifex Ferry, on the Gauley River, in time to prepare our camp before night.

Soon after our arrival Captain Schutte, of Company K, was on picket duty at Carnifex Ferry. During the day the captain, for some unknown reason, conceived the idea of a scout across the river. Selecting fourteen of his men, he crossed over to the opposite bank, and, taking the main road, immediately pushed into the country. The march was made, apparently, without any apprehension of the presence of an enemy; at least, no steps appear to have been taken to prevent a surprise. All went well, however, until the party had made a distance of several miles, when, the first intimation they had of danger, they were fired upon by a party of cavalry, concealed in an adjacent thicket, and all but four of the party killed or wounded—Captain Schutte being wounded mortally. The survivors conveyed him to an old building, and, at his own request, left him. He expired soon after, and was buried on the spot by the rebels. The four men fled towards the river, and, being pursued, took to the woods. One, being separated from his companions, was pursued to the bank of the river, and was only saved by throwing himself into the stream from the projecting rocks. He concealed his body under water, keeping sufficient of his face above to sustain life. He could plainly distinguish the conversation of the rebels, and knew by it that they were in search of him. Here he remained during the day, and at night dragged himself upon the rocks. The next morning, tired and hungry, he floated himself down stream by clinging to the almost perpendicular rocks, until, arriving opposite a house, he was hailed by a woman, to whom he made known his condition. She immediately unfastened a canoe, and, paddling directly across the river to where he was lying, half famished in the water, helped him over its sides, and conveyed him to the other shore. Before they landed, however, the rebels discovered them, and gave the order to "halt." It not being obeyed, they fired, the bullets sinking harmlessly into the water. In a moment the two were lost to view in the pau-pau, which lined the river bank. The woman guided the soldier to her home, where she cared for him during a short illness, which succeeded his escape. When he was sufficiently recovered to join his command, he found the regiment had abandoned Cross Lanes, which had been occupied by the rebel forces. He returned to his former retreat, where he was concealed until the day of the disaster to the Seventh, when, taking advantage of the confusion into which the rebel forces were thrown during the affair, he escaped towards Gauley Bridge, which place he reached in safety the following day.

CHAPTER IV.

The skirmish at Cross Lanes.—Gallant conduct and final escape of the Seventh Regiment.

The occupation of Cross Lanes was considered by the authorities of the gravest importance. It was contiguous to three fords on the Gauley River, which, when possessed by the Federal forces, was a perfect protection to the left of the army occupying Gauley Bridge. Carnifex Ferry was immediately south two and one-half miles. There was a road leading from the vicinity of Gauley Bridge, on the south bank of the Gauley River, which unites with the Sunday road, crossing the river at this ferry. This road afforded the enemy a means of gaining the left of our forces, at Gauley Bridge. The occupation of Cross Lanes, therefore, by the enemy, would sever the communication between our forces at the above point, and the main army under Rosecrans, occupying the country from the Baltimore and Ohio Railroad, along Cheat Mountain.

Carnifex Ferry, was a point easily defended against a much superior force. Indeed, it had so many natural defences, that it elicited exclamations of surprise from men accustomed to the selection of places for defence. The current of the river was rapid, while the abrupt rocks on its banks afforded secure hiding places for a considerable body of troops. It was quite impossible to bring artillery to bear in such a manner on the position as to interfere materially with troops concealed there. It seems to be the opinion of most persons familiar with the place, that it would be quite impossible to dislodge a body of troops properly posted on the north bank of the river at this ferry, provided a stubborn resistance was made.

It was for the purpose of preventing the crossing of the enemy at this point that the force of Colonel Tyler was ordered to Cross Lanes. By keeping pickets well on the line of the river, to watch any advance of the enemy, the regiment was entirely safe at its camp, from which it was comparatively easy to re-enforce any portion of the line. But for some reason, the commanding officer failed to visit the ferry in person, until the afternoon of the day on which a peremptory order was received to report with his command at Gauley Bridge. Hitherto he had been entirely unable to give correct information, as to the probability of his being able to hold the ferry. He was ordered to abandon the position, because his dispatches were such, that they created an uneasiness in the minds of Generals Rosecrans and Cox, as to the propriety of trusting him to hold so important a position. Here was the fatal mistake. A lesser error had already been made, in withdrawing all the forces from Tyler, other than the Seventh. Had these forces remained, the position would probably not have been abandoned, as all would have felt secure. When the order to withdraw was received, the commanding officer regretted it as much as any one. But the mischief was already done; the order was imperative. On that evening, Monday, the regiment left Cross Lanes at 11 o'clock P.M., and the next day, by noon, was at Twenty Mile Creek, some eight miles from Gauley Bridge.

On the Wednesday morning following, Colonel Tyler reported in person to General Cox. In the mean time, the general having become satisfied that Colonel Tyler could be trusted to hold Cross Lanes, and being confident that the contemplated attack of the enemy on Gauley Bridge had been abandoned, ordered him to return as soon as the troops were rested, expecting him to start back, at least the next morning. But Tyler did not move. On Friday afternoon, General Cox, on learning that he had not moved, was much excited, and said to an officer present—

"He must move; he must move at once; it is all important that Cross Lanes be held, and Floyd be kept on the other side of the river; ride back to camp and tell him from me, to move early in the morning, *and with speed, to secure the position*."

The order was delivered in nearly the same language as given, but notwithstanding its directness, he did not move till noon on Saturday, and then made a distance of only fourteen miles, over good roads, encamping at the foot of Panther Mountain, after having fallen back from Peter's Creek, on learning of the presence of the enemy.

On arriving in camp, a dispatch was sent to General Cox, representing to him that the enemy were in force in front, and asking instructions. On Sunday morning at about 3 o'clock, a courier arrived with an order from General Cox, substantially as follows: The force in your front cannot be as large as you estimate it. Advance cautiously, feeling your way; if the enemy is too strong, fall back, if not, occupy Cross Lanes at once, as it is of the utmost importance.

About nine o'clock Sunday morning, August 25th, the regiment moved towards Cross Lanes, casting lots as to which company should be left in charge of the baggage. It fell upon Company F, which was temporarily commanded by Lieutenant Kimball. The entire day was occupied in reaching Cross Lanes. It was not until dark of that day that the regiment went into camp.

In the days' advance some slight skirmishing occurred with the enemy's cavalry videttes, but beyond these few horsemen no enemy was encountered, the regiment encamping in apparent security near the church, after having driven away a cavalry picket of the enemy.

Companies were sent out on picket, as follows: Company A, on the road leading to Summerville; Company K, on the road leading to Carnifex Ferry; Company C, on the road leading in the opposite direction, while Company E was sent on a diagonal road leading to a ferry some distance below Carnifex. The balance of the command remained near headquarters, which were established in the church.

Each company on picket was divided into three reliefs, with instructions to be vigilant.

The silence of the enemy, together with his neglect to attack, created the impression that he had withdrawn his forces to the other side of the river, fearing that this small force was but the advance of a well-equipped army. But these theories were destined to fade into sadder realities, as the shadows of night melted into morning.

Nothing occurred during the night to disturb the general repose. A short time before day fires were kindled, and those who were up had pieces of meat on sticks, which they were roasting. Some had obtained green corn during the night, which they were also roasting. Before day had fairly dawned, the command was almost entirely astir. As it became sufficiently light to distinguish objects at a considerable distance, several musket shots were heard in the direction of the river, followed in quick succession by others. It soon became evident that a determined attack was being made on Company K. About this time a column of rebels was seen advancing from the river road, across the fields, towards Company A's position on the Summerville road. Arriving in the vicinity of this road, the column halted, formed in line of battle, at the same time swinging round its right to the Summerville road, driving Company A back to the point where the roads cross. In the mean time Companies B, D, G, H, and I were ordered to the support of Company K; but on arriving at the cross roads, Company K was seen falling back in some confusion, before a superior force, therefore they remained at that point. Meanwhile a heavy fire was opened from a dense wood opposite the church, to resist which Company K, having been joined by Companies A and C, which had advanced to its support on the ferry road, took position on a hill midway between this belt of timber and the crossing of the roads. From this point these companies delivered several effective volleys, which soon drove the rebels from their position. Taking advantage of this partial check of the enemy, Captain Crane ordered a charge, which resulted in piercing the lines, and the capture of a stand of rebel colors. The three companies now escaped, with a loss, however, of Captain Shurtliff, Lieutenant Wilcox, and Lieutenant Cross, taken prisoners, the latter being severely wounded in the arm.

During this time the rebel column from the direction of Summerville had advanced so as to lap over the road opposite the Ferry road, exposing the companies occupying the road in front of the church to an enfilading fire, at the same time being exposed to a severe fire from the front, from a column of infantry and cavalry coming up the Ferry road. These companies were now ordered to rally on a hill near the church. In executing this movement Companies D and H passed through a corn field, exposed to a deadly fire from almost every direction. Soon after reaching this field Captain Dyer, Company D, fell dead, pierced in the heart by a rifle bullet. Lieutenant Weed succeeded him in command. On reaching the hill these companies attempted to rally, but being in an open field, combated by a much superior and partially hidden foe, were compelled to fall back to a piece of woods skirting the road. The balance of the command, other than those who had followed the fortunes of Captain Crane, now joined them, and soon organized for a systematic retreat.

Captain Crane and his followers, after putting some distance between themselves and the enemy, crossed the Gauley road, and hastened to the mountains, where they would be entirely free from the attacks of cavalry, and where they would have a chance, at least, of partially defending themselves against attack from the rebel infantry.

Arriving in the mountains, they took a direction as nearly as possible towards Gauley Bridge, where they arrived in safety, meeting with little of adventure on the way. Thus a small body of Federals had fought their way out from the very grasp of the enemy, and, eluding pursuit, traversed a mountain range, with no guide, over rocks and deep gorges, arriving safely within the Union lines. Their arrival, however, did little to cheer the hearts of those in camp, for they were a small body compared with those still unheard from.

The news of the sad disaster to the Seventh had already been sent to the friends at home; universal gloom had settled over the camp, and the prospect looked dark for saving the organization, even, of a regiment which was the pride of the Western Reserve.

A flag of truce was sent to Cross Lanes to ascertain, if possible, the fate of those left behind. Chaplain Brown and Surgeon Cushing were selected to undertake this enterprise. They, however, returned without having accomplished their object.

One dark, rainy night, as if nature was in sympathy with the feelings of those in camp, the band commenced playing a patriotic air in front of the colonel's quarters, accompanied with cheers. I knew that this indicated good news. Hastening to the spot I learned that a dispatch had just arrived from Charleston with the comforting news that four hundred of the regiment had arrived in safety on the Elk River, twelve miles from the above place. But let us accompany these four hundred heroes in their march from the battlefield.

Organizing the troops, Major Casement, being first in rank, Colonels Tyler and Creighton having already escaped, assumed command. Losing no time the detachment immediately took up the line of march. Avoiding all highways, and keeping well in the timber, they moved on for some time, when, considering themselves out of immediate danger, they ventured out to the road, to find themselves only three miles from the place of starting. It was now concluded that it was not advisable to attempt reaching Gauley Bridge, as the enemy would be likely to interpose a considerable body of troops between them and that point. It was considered to be more practicable to make in the direction of Elk River, and by this means reach Charleston. This course being adopted, the command crossed the road and took to the mountains. Very soon after a party of rebel cavalry came dashing down as if in pursuit, barely missing the object of their search.

The command, aided by a compass, took their course over the mountains in a direction which they supposed would ultimately lead them to the banks of the Elk

River.

During the afternoon Captain W. R. Sterling procured a guide, who conducted them by narrow pathways, in which they were compelled to march single file, towards a house which was situated at some distance on the mountain. Night setting in, before reaching the spot, without even a star visible to light them on the way, the column halted, and passed the word back for a candle. The line extended for nearly half a mile, and it was not until the last company, H, had been reached, that one was procured. On its arriving at the front, it was discovered that the head of the column had arrived on the brink of a deep chasm, into which it would be sure death to plunge. One step more, and the unlucky leader of the line would have been precipitated into the dreadful crater. But these daring adventurers were spared the misfortune of such an accident.

Two hours of valuable time having been lost, the line now pressed forward, each man holding on to the man preceding him. About midnight the house was reached, and the weary band laid themselves down; not, however, to sleep, for the only provisions they had had during the day was roasted corn, for in the morning they were attacked while preparing breakfast, which they were compelled to abandon. The woman of the house was kept cooking the good old-fashioned corn-dodger, and by morning the command was tolerably well fed, and ready for the toilsome as well as hazardous march of the succeeding day.

As the day again dawned, the line moved on. Procuring another guide during the day, they arrived, in early evening, on the banks of the Elk River, without any adventure worth relating. Before halting they forded the river, which was, at the time, waist deep. Company B was sent out on picket, under command of Lieutenant Molyneaux. The instructions were to establish a chain of pickets, at short intervals, along the road leading up the river. In case of an attack, the outer picket to fire and fall back on the next, when another volley was to be delivered, and so continue until the camp should be finally reached. The position selected for the camp was at the base of a range of abrupt hills, which were not accessible to cavalry, while many difficulties would present themselves in the way of a force of infantry advancing to an attack from that direction. The river ran at the very foot of these hills, too deep to cross in the face of an enemy, and sufficiently wide to present a decided obstacle in the way of an attacking party on the opposite shore. The command felt, therefore, comparatively safe in this retreat. As it afterwards proved, they were not mistaken; for it was ascertained that, at the time the pickets were being stationed, seven hundred rebel cavalry were a short distance up the river; indeed, they were so near that a party of rebel officers heard the lieutenant give the instructions to the outer picket. One of these officers, when afterwards taken prisoner, being questioned by Molyneaux as to their reason for not attacking, remarked that it would have been quite impossible for them to reach the camp in case his instructions to the picket should be carried out; and he and his brother-officers agreed in the opinion, that the orders would be carried out; for no body of troops, after having made so stubborn a resistance as at Cross Lanes, would afterwards lose all by a want of vigilance or a disobedience of orders. True it is that they did not attack, but suffered the camp to remain quiet, and the command to move off at leisure in the morning.

A dispatch being sent to Charleston, on the following day a provision-train met them twelve miles from the latter place. In due time the command arrived at Charleston, weary and foot-sore from their long and toilsome march.

CHAPTER V.

Reflections on the Skirmish at Cross Lanes.—Battle of Carnifex Ferry.

The occasion for the affair at Cross Lanes was brought about by a series of blunders. The first blunder was committed by the officer who ordered all the forces, with the exception of the Seventh Ohio, from a position which enabled them to guard the ferries of the Gauley. If it was deemed important to hold these ferries at all, it was certainly advisable to retain a sufficient force to guard against surprise and capture. But then, what would be considered a sufficient force? To settle the question, it is necessary to take into account the size of the army occupying the country, as well as the size of that of the enemy. Neither army was large, and both were much scattered, scarcely more than a brigade occupying one position. A regiment, therefore, may perhaps be considered a sufficient force for an outpost.

The army in Western Virginia was at no time sufficiently large to accomplish any thing, under the best generalship, beyond simply holding the country, and preventing invasion; and it was only for the want of a moderately sized army that the rebel general failed to drive back our forces. But the rebel authorities had no men to spare for the purpose of winning barren victories; so the armies of Western Virginia were left to watch each other, with an occasional skirmish.

At the time the affair at Cross Lanes took place, our army occupied a front of many miles, as did also the rebel army. It was quite impossible to collect, in case of emergency, more than about six thousand men. But, however it may be as to the first point, it is clear, secondly, that the commanding officer at Cross Lanes committed an error in not making a personal inspection of the grounds, adjacent to the camp, immediately on his arrival. It is always considered highly important that those in command should know precisely the ground their commands are expected to defend, and not to trust to chance or a battle to develop favorable points of defence or attack. By reason of this want of knowledge, rumors as to the presence of the enemy in force created uneasiness and alarm, which was entirely natural, although without cause. While in this state of feeling, the commanding officer sent dispatches to Generals Rosecrans and Cox, which created the impression that their author was not to be trusted to hold these ferries. Those generals attributed this alarm to a want of personal courage, they being well informed as to the strength of the position at Cross Lanes. It was not, however, a want of courage, but simply a failure on his part to understand the real strength of the position, by reason of not having visited it in person.

When the order to withdraw came, Colonel Tyler regretted it as much as any one; for he had that day examined the position, and knew that he could hold it against any force the enemy could bring to the attack. But this knowledge was obtained too late: lying on his table was a positive order to withdraw. Reason said hold the position; military law, which was higher in authority, said abandon it; so the place was evacuated. The third and irremediable error was committed in not returning to Cross Lanes when ordered. If that had been done, the consequences resulting from the withdrawal would have been entirely checked. The order to return was given on Wednesday, with the expectation that it would be acted upon as soon as Thursday morning; but it was not until the Saturday noon following that the command started. There was no reason for this delay. The regiment had marched but eighteen miles in as many days, and could, without any injustice being done it, have returned the day the order was given. Even had the command moved as late as Friday, with dispatch, it would not have been too late, as it seems to be well settled that Floyd did not cross over any considerable body of troops until Saturday.

In the way of criticism on this affair, it has been said that, had a spirited dash been made on the enemy on Saturday evening, the rebels could have been driven across the river. I think this claim subject to many doubts. In my opinion a reconnoissance should have been made that night, instead of falling back to Panther Mountain. This would have resulted in the discovery of their position and force, and thus given the command an opportunity to take advantage of the night to withdraw. Had this been done, the ferry might possibly have been reached.

The result of these blunders was the fighting of two engagements, with a heavy Federal loss, while the enemy suffered less. One of these, Carnifex Ferry, has been dignified with the name of battle, while the other is considered but an affair.

After the repulse of the Seventh, Floyd intrenched himself on the bank of the river, near the ferry. About two weeks later, "Rosecrans came down with his legions," comprising about four thousand men. Approaching the vicinity of the ferry, he threw forward General Benham's brigade, with no design of bringing on an engagement, however; but the line unwittingly advanced to within a short distance of the enemy's works, when a sheet of flame shot along their entire line. The unequal contest lasted five hours, when the Union forces withdrew, hungry and supperless, with a loss of fourteen killed, and one hundred and four wounded. The loss of the enemy was about twenty wounded.

The troops awoke in the morning to find the rebel works abandoned. Thus ended the battle of Carnifex Ferry, no less a blunder than Cross Lanes.

General Benham was censured for having attacked their main works, when he was ordered to make a reconnoissance only. But when it is understood that the commanding general sent up reinforcements, the blame, if there was any, attached itself to him.

The loss to the Seventh, at Cross Lanes, was one killed, twenty wounded, and ninety-six taken prisoners. Several of these were recaptured at Carnifex Ferry, when Rosecrans attacked Floyd. Among the number was Lieutenant Cross, Company C. The loss to the enemy has never been known. There is no doubt, however, that it was considerable. They attacked in large numbers, confident of an easy victory, therefore very little caution attended their movements. But instead of a flag of truce, accompanied by an offer to surrender, they were met by a shower of bullets, which must have told fearfully on their heavy columns. The fact that they were thrown into such confusion as to permit our men to escape, shows that they were too severely punished to follow up their victory.

The force of Floyd has been variously estimated: some having placed it as high as six thousand; while, in his official report of the engagement at Carnifex Ferry, Floyd himself places it at only two thousand. His force was probably four thousand, of all arms, with ten pieces of artillery. This entire force must have been in the vicinity at the time of the affair at Cross Lanes.

The following is an unofficial list of the loss in the regiment:

Killed.—Captain John N. Dyer.

Wounded.—Corporal Frank Dutton, N. J. Holly, Thomas Shepley, Thomas J. Scoville, Sergeant H. G. Orton, Joseph W. Collins, B. Yeakins, Lewis J. Jones, Thomas S. Curran, William Meriman, B. F. Gill, William S. Reed, David M. Daily, Robert J. Furguson, James R. Greer, E. J. Kreiger, Sergeant James Grebe, John W. Doll, William W. Ritiche, Fred. W. Steinbauer.

The following is a list of those taken prisoners:

Sergeant W. W. Parmeter, Sergeant E. R. Stiles, Sergeant G. C. C. Ketchum, Sergeant F. F. Wilcoxson, Sergeant Edward Bohn, Sergeant A. Kolman, Sergeant E. W. Morey, Corporal C. F. Mack, Corporal J. G. Turner, Corporal T. A. Mohler, Corporal S. M. Cole, Corporal E. C. Palmer, Corporal Charles Bersett, Privates Albert Osborn, Charles Weber, Alex. Parker, R. Bears, L. Warren, A. M. Halbert, H. Keiser, S. B. Kingsbury, E. Kennedy, A. Hubbell, C. C. Quinn, C. Burrows, E. Evans, W. H. Scott, C. H. Howard, Charles Carrol, T. B. Myers, George Sweet, John Massa, J. F. Curtis, W. E. Bartlett, W. Cherry, John Bark, John Hann, L. M. Blakesly, Z. Fox, J. Butler, F. S. Stillwell, G. W. Downing, G. C. Newton, William Biggs, Mathew Merkle, J. Sheloy, H. Huntoon, G. W. Williams, George C. Robinson, H. Wessenbock, J. C. Rafferty, J. Snyder, W. W. Wheeler, C. Haskell, J. W. Finch, James Johnson, H. Johnson, L. C. Logue, A. Scoville, P. Wildson, F. Boole, John Miller, P. Jenkins, John Smith, J. Wolf, Theodore Burt, A. Schwartz, G. A. Akerman, Charles Sahl, G. W. Thompson, F. Williams, M. H. Whaley, Z. Larkins, T. Hebbig, Z. A. Fuig, F. A. Noble, J. Hettlick, J. McCabe, L. Beles, E. R. Smith, F. A. Rubicon, John Smith, E. Smith, H. Smith, D. N. K. Hubbard, H. Wood, Charles Ottinger, R. S. Beel, N. D. Claghorn, H. Thompson, N. Freidenburg, M. Levullen, S. Gill, fifer.

CHAPTER VI.

Charleston and the Kanawha Valley.—A double murder.—Colonel Tyler assumes command of the post.

After the engagement at Cross Lanes, five companies of the regiment remained at Gauley Bridge, while the balance were at Charleston. The latter part was commanded by Colonel Guthrie, of the First Kentucky Regiment. At this time it was the seat of justice for Kanawha County, and contained upwards of three thousand inhabitants. It is a neat village, situated on the north bank of the Kanawha River, at a point where the Elk empties into it. There is a fine suspension bridge over the latter stream, which the rebels undertook to destroy in their flight. Charleston is three hundred and eight miles west of Richmond, and forty-six miles east of the Ohio River. It was named after Charles Clendenin, an early settler, and an owner of the soil on which it is built.

The Valley of the Kanawha is famous for its beautiful scenery. The mountains on either side of the river sometimes rise to the height of five hundred feet and more, and are liberally supplied with rich beds of minerals and coal. At their base is located the famous Kanawha salt works. They commence near Charleston, and extend for about fifteen miles above it. Before the rebellion they gave employment to nearly six thousand persons. The following extract will be of interest:

"It is a curious fact, and worthy of philosophical inquiry, that while the salt water is obtained by boring to a depth of from three hundred to five hundred feet below the bed of the Kanawha, it invariably rises to a level with the river. When the latter is swollen by rains, or the redundant waters of its tributaries, the saline fluid, inclosed in suitable "gums" on the shore, ascends like the mercury in its tube, and only falls when the river returns to its wonted channel. How this mysterious correspondence is produced is a problem which remains to be solved. Theories and speculations I have heard on the subject, but none seem to me to be precisely consonant with the principles of science."

Before the presence of the army interrupted the manufacture of salt, these works yielded about two million bushels annually, and are capable of yielding much more with an increase of capital.

While Colonel Guthrie commanded the post at Charleston a most disgraceful tragedy was enacted. An order had been issued that no liquors of any description should be sold or given to the soldiers or employees of the Government. During the time this order was in force, a party of drunken rowdies from the First Kentucky Regiment stopped at the grocery of an old man, and asked for some beer; when refused, they demanded it. Being again refused they threatened violence, and proceeded to put their threats into force, when a son of the old man, occupying a room above, was brought to the window by the old gentleman's cries for help, and, seeing his father thus set upon by a mob, from the repeated assaults of which his life was endangered, fired a revolver, the contents of which took effect on one of the assaulting party, producing instant death. He was at once arrested and lodged in jail, around which a strong guard was placed to prevent his being taken out and hung.

That night Colonel Guthrie, in a speech made to the excited throng, which had collected around the jail, said, in substance, that the life of the criminal should be taken if he had to do it with his own hand. Similar remarks were made by others, among whom was a captain who afterwards sat as judge-advocate on the trial.

On the morning after the affair the members constituting the court-martial assembled "in all the pomp and pride of glorious war," decorated with all the paraphernalia belonging to an officer's equipment, but to declare a prejudged opinion.

During the trial the prisoner was as immovable as a statue, evincing in his appearance a want of hope, as well as a preparation for the worst. He made no defence. The announcement of the sentence of death produced no change; he preserved a stoical appearance to the last.

When the hour of execution arrived the prisoner was brought to the gallows in a heavy wagon, guarded by a double file of soldiers, who were laughing as gayly as if on their way to some place of amusement. During the afternoon the sun had shone through a cloudless sky; but just before this terrible scene was enacted, the heavens were draped with heavy clouds, and the rain fell in torrents, casting a gloom on all around. The wretched victim ascended the gallows with a firm tread, and addressed a few words, in a fearless tone, to those assembled around. As the rope was being adjusted around his neck, the crowd involuntarily gave way, showing that, although they had been clamorous for the enactment of the scene, yet when the time came, they had not the nerve to witness the death-struggle of their victim. There was but little movement of the body after the fatal drop fell. This last scene was sickening in the extreme, and all of us, moved by a common impulse, turned and walked away in silence, our hearts being too full for utterance.

This is one more testimony against the safety and justice of the death penalty.

On the 19th day of October, Colonel Tyler took command of the post at Charleston. He issued the following proclamation:

"In assuming the command of this post, one of my principal objects will be to maintain order, and to see that the rights of persons and property have the protection guaranteed by general orders from department headquarters. To the faithful execution of this my entire energies, together with the force at my command, will be given. To this end I have established Camp Warren, where officers and soldiers are required to be at all times, except when on duty which calls them away, or on leave of absence, which will only be granted at headquarters. Commissioned and non-commissioned officers will be held personally responsible for any violation of this order by members of their companies. Drunkenness, marauding, boisterous and unsoldierlike conduct are strictly forbidden. To prevent this, the sale of intoxicating liquors, directly or indirectly, to those in the service of the United States, is positively and emphatically prohibited; and I call upon the citizens to aid me in detecting those who violate this order. The quiet of your town, the protection of your property—in fact your lives and the lives of your families—depend much upon the sobriety of our officers and men; therefore, it becomes your duty as well as your interest to lend me your aid in the execution of this order.

"E. B. Tyler,
"Colonel Commanding Post."

Under the rule of Colonel Tyler the post at Charleston assumed order and quiet. Under the former commandant drunkenness was common, while marauding parties were free to patrol the streets on their errands of mischief. The property of the citizens was at the mercy of these gangs, while their lives were not unfrequently placed in jeopardy. The people, therefore, were much gratified with the change of rule. Camps were now established at some distance from the village, while no soldiers were permitted to visit it unless they first obtained a pass from headquarters, which, being established in town, was difficult to procure. A provost-marshal was appointed, with a proper guard subject to his orders. This guard was instructed to arrest all soldiers found in the streets of the village without a proper pass, as well as those committing any depredations on the property or persons of the citizens, with or without a pass.

About the middle of October the companies at Gauley Bridge came down to Charleston. During their stay on the Gauley they performed much duty at the outposts; several times being under the enemy's fire, though none were injured. The detachment suffered severe loss, however, from sickness. Lieutenant Robinson was among the number; he died of fever; his loss was greatly felt by the regiment. When the news of his death reached his company, they wept as for a brother.

CHAPTER VII.

Floyd establishes batteries on Cotton Hill.—Driven off by the forces of general Cox.—Benham's failure to intercept his retreat.—His pursuit.—Skirmish at McCoy's Mills.—His final escape.

Near the last of October General Floyd very suddenly appeared on Cotton Hill, an abrupt eminence lying between the Kanawha and New rivers, at the junction of the Gauley with the latter stream, which form the Kanawha. The enemy immediately commenced shelling Gauley Bridge. General Cox, who was some distance up New River, near the headquarters of General Rosecrans, was ordered to proceed to Gauley Bridge and to assume direction of affairs. He was also ordered to direct General Benham, who was expected to arrive very soon with a brigade, to cross his forces, at night, over the Kanawha River, and to carry the summit of Cotton Hill by storm. A picket post had already been established across the river by direction of General Cox. Benham protested against the movement, and refused to execute the order received through General Cox, but proceeded to confer, by telegraph, with General Rosecrans, receiving in reply the same orders. Benham still protesting against attempting to execute what he termed so hazardous a movement, at his own request was permitted to pass down the river to the mouth of Loop Creek, from whence he was to undertake a flank movement. Colonel Smith joined General Benham in his protest, declaring the attempt to storm these batteries as sheer madness. It is significant that General Cox afterwards stormed and carried Cotton Hill, with barely a regiment of troops.

Floyd had constructed a line of fortifications at Dickerson's, on the road to

Fayetteville, which was his only avenue of retreat in case of disaster.

Soon after General Benham arrived opposite Loop Creek, he was joined by five hundred selected men from the Seventh from Charleston. This detachment of the regiment, having arrived on boats, was ordered to disembark, and take up their position at the mouth of Loop Creek. The following morning it moved up the creek some eight or ten miles, where it took up its position at an old log barn. Lieutenant-Colonel Creighton being in command, Colonel Tyler having remained at Charleston, was instructed to picket the roads well in his front, as well as the mountains lying between; and also to scout the country in the vicinity, for the purpose of finding out the position of the camp of the enemy, as well as his numbers. The latter part of the order was well executed, and there can be no doubt that Benham was possessed of accurate information of the enemy.

After the third day of our occupation of this position we were joined by a detachment of the Forty-fourth Ohio, under command of Major Mitchell, and the Thirty-seventh Ohio, under command of Colonel Seibert. Soon after, all of this force, with the exception of eight companies of the Thirty-seventh Regiment, was ordered forward under command of Lieutenant-Colonel Creighton.

Proceeding for some distance on a road leading to the front, we struck into a bridle path, and after passing through a wood, began ascending a mountain. Single file, the command clambered up its steep and rocky sides. Arriving on its summit we could see the heads of a line of men extending for a mile beneath us. Descending the opposite side with some difficulty, we marched some distance from the foot of the mountain, and found ourselves at Cassady's Mills, a point from which the command was to debouch on to the Fayetteville pike, should Floyd attempt a retreat. But the movement, on the part of Benham, was so tardily executed, that the balance of the command never arrived at this point; but instead, the forces, other than the Seventh Ohio, were ordered away that night; leaving a detachment of five hundred men, with no support, within three miles of a well-equipped army of the enemy. We were so near that we could plainly hear the bugle calls in Floyd's camp. Had Benham's entire command been at that point, the retreat of the rebel army could have been intercepted. Previous to this, Floyd had been driven back to his intrenchments at Dickerson's, and all that was necessary to his capture, was an attack on his rear on the part of Benham. But he either feared to make the attack, or was too slow in doing it. The former is probably true. That night the rebel general passed within three miles of our position, and escaped with his entire army, together with the artillery and baggage.

On the 12th of November, Benham arrived at Cotton Hill, but to find the forces of General Cox in possession. On the afternoon of the 13th, he pushed on after Floyd's retreating army, arriving within four miles of Fayetteville, at about eleven o'clock P.M. Here, evidences of the hurried retreat of Floyd began to multiply. The fences were lined with hides, but recently stripped from the carcasses of cattle, while in many places the beef itself was left suspended from the fence.

On the morning of the 4th, we pushed through Fayetteville before day, in the pursuit. Floyd had but a few hours the start. Six miles ahead we took breakfast, consisting of two army crackers to each man. After which we pushed rapidly on. About noon, our skirmishers, the Thirteenth Ohio, overtook the rear-guard of the enemy, when sharp firing occurred, which continued during an advance of several miles, resulting in the mortal wounding of St. George Croghan, colonel of the Second Georgia cavalry, and formerly of the United States Army. The colonel was taken to a house close by and left, where he was found in a dying condition by our men. Having been a class-mate of his at West Point, Benham stopped and passed a few words with him. When recognizing the general, Croghan appeared to be much affected; and is reported to have said that he knew he was fighting in a bad cause, and that he had been driven into the army much against his wishes, for he was still attached to the old flag. He soon after expired.

While this conversation was being carried on between officers so differently circumstanced, the Union forces had pressed the rebels so closely, that the latter, to save their baggage train, were compelled to make a stand. The Seventh Ohio was ordered to act as reserve, but when the action grew hot, was ordered forward, with instructions to send out two companies as skirmishers, which was immediately done; Companies A and K being sent forward.

About this time two pieces of rifled cannon were brought to bear on the rebels, when they turned and fled, leaving six killed on the field. We were so near, that we plainly heard the retreat sounded by their bugles. From this time their retreat became a rout. In their flight, they cast away every thing that would encumber their retreat. We were now on the banks of a stream, over whose rocky cliffs numerous wagons, with their contents, had been hurled. It was supposed, that several pieces of cannon shared the same fate.

The pursuit was continued with much vigor, until a late hour in the evening, when General Schenck, having but just arrived at the front, ordered it discontinued. This was the second error of the campaign. Schenck, with his fresh troops, instead of ordering the pursuit to cease, should have pressed with vigor. The enemy encamped but a short distance in our front, on Three-mile Mountain. This position could have been carried with ease, with the combined forces of Schenck and Benham, with comparatively little loss. But the pursuit being the result of a blunder, resulted in a blunder.

A little after midnight the command fell back, arriving at Fayetteville in the afternoon of the same day, after a fatiguing march over the worst road that could be imagined, and with no provisions other than beef with a very little salt. The Seventh marched to its old camp, four miles out on the road to Cotton Hill. The officers and men lay on the hill-side that night, exposed to a violent snow storm, with no other covering than their blankets, except the snowy sheet that nature spread over them during the long hours of night.

During the night a demonstration was made on a drove of pigs which were lurking close by; and it would not be strange if the soldiers could relate tales of their descent on poultry yards and bee-hives. True it is, that some first-class honey found its way into camp.

The next day, marching over Cotton Hill, we arrived at our camp near the mouth of Loop Creek. Embarking on the following day, we arrived at Charleston on the 18th, after an absence of fourteen days.

CHAPTER VIII.

Reflections on the Institution of Slavery.

While at Charleston, we were deeply impressed with the profound interest the slaves were taking in passing events. That down-trodden race, who had for years suffered every injustice at the hands of their white oppressors, were now the first to assist the Federal commanders. Through darkness and storm, they carried information, and acted as scouts and guides on occasions when it would try the heart and nerve of their white companions.

From my own observation, I am confident that the slaves of the South, were just as well informed with regard to their relation to their masters, as we were. They were, from the very first, impressed with the idea that this rebellion was to work some great change in their condition. They were watching, with great interest, every movement of troops, and were continually asking questions, as to the disposition to be made of them; thus evincing an interest in military affairs, of which their masters little dreamed. It is well enough to talk of the deep devotion of slaves to their masters; but the latter have found ere this, I trust, that this devotion on which they have relied, has not prevented them from cutting their throats, when it was in the line of their duty, and by means of which they could gain their freedom. An instance of this great devotion on the part of a slave for his master, was related to me while at Charleston.

A Mr. R—— owned a colored servant by the name of John; he enjoyed the unlimited confidence of his master, who was in the habit of trusting him as he would one of his children. This confidence was reciprocated by a like devotion on the part of the slave for his master. One day a neighbor told Mr. R—— that his John was about to run away, as he had repeated conversations with his servants on the subject. Mr. R—— flew into a passion, feeling very much grieved that his neighbor should think, for a moment, that his John, whom he had raised from infancy, should prove so ungrateful as to leave him. The only attention he paid to this timely warning was, to put still greater trust in his servant. One day, shortly after this, John was missing; not only this, he had been so ungrateful as to take his wife and three children. The last heard from faithful John was, that he was safe in Ohio. Now Mr. R—— is a very good man and a Christian, and treat his servants very kindly; but that God-given principle, a desire for personal liberty, actuated him in connection with other men of fairer complexion. John, undoubtedly, left his old home and master with regret, but home and friendship, when compared with freedom, were nothing.

I was once told by a colored man, in whom the utmost confidence could be placed, that there has been for years an association among the negroes, which extends throughout the South, the purpose of which was one day to liberate themselves from slavery. He said that hundreds of slaves who, apparently, were as innocent as ignorant, were tolerably well educated, and were secretly bending every energy to bring about an insurrection, which should end in their being released from bondage. When asked if the field-hands were members of this association, he said they were; and although possessing less information than those living in the cities and villages, yet they were aware of what was going on; and after their work was done at night, they often met in their cabins, and talked over the prospect before them. He also said, that in the larger cities of the South this association had regular meetings and officers; that they awaited only the proper time, when a tragedy would be enacted all over the South, that would astonish the world.

When we reflect that revolts have been common in the South, and that they have been attended by partial success, it does not require a great stretch of the imagination to believe that this association did really exist. The fact of the intense feeling of hatred cherished by the people of the South against Northern fanatics, as they were termed, who came amongst them, is strong evidence in favor of the existence of some organized course of policy among the negroes. The outward appearance of the slave is usually gentle in the extreme, although his inward feelings may be agitated to such a degree, that in a white man they would burst forth in the wildest passion. Therefore, this hatred of the South to the opponents of slavery must be traced to a fear of some secret organization, the object of which lay deeply buried in the reticent minds of the slaves. The Southern mind was more deeply agitated, from the fact of the want of this outward emotion on the part of their slaves; for had this strong desire for liberty, which was awakened in them, burst out in wild enthusiasm, it would have been readily checked by the severe punishment of individuals; but it was this secret working of this deep-laid desire for freedom that troubled them. The most guilty were, to all outward appearance, the most innocent.

While the Federal army occupied the country, the slaves were much less guarded in what they said. One of these slaves, an old man, was passing a tent one day, when a soldier said to him that he belonged to Jeff. Davis. With a knowing look, he replied: "I did; but now, massa, I belong to Uncle Sam." A colored woman, who had been a slave for years (as she is very old), came into our room one day, and taking up a paper, asked if we wanted it. Some one said to her, as she was about leaving the room, that she had better not be seen with that paper, as it was not the sort her mistress admired. Said she, "I know what missus likes; I can take care of it;" and slipping it under her apron she left the room. That slave could read and write, and yet her master knew nothing of it. So it is with many others. It may be asked how they acquire this knowledge. They gain it in a great many ways. Many of them learn of their masters' children, with whom house-servants spend a great deal of time. Having acquired a slight knowledge, it stimulates them to greater exertion. They obtain scraps of newspapers and parts of books, and thus gain a great deal of information entirely unobserved. The slave knows how to keep secrets; consequently, any scheme that is on foot is seldom discovered. Few persons, at the commencement of the rebellion, had the least conception of the vast resources and power of the slave population of the South. And it was not until they had fed and clothed the Southern armies for two years, and by this means kept them in the field, that it was acknowledged. Had it not been for its slaves, the South, long ere this, would have been compelled to yield obedience to the Government. The rebels appreciated and used this element of strength from the beginning. The Federal Government, through the influence of weak-minded politicians, rejected it; thus throwing an element of its own strength into the hands of its enemies.

Notwithstanding this harsh treatment, the slaves proved true to the Government; and finally, through the medium of this faithfulness, their vast services were acknowledged, and they have not only been taken into the private service of the country, but they have been admitted into the army, to swell its numbers, until the strength of their mighty arms, and the nerve of their fearless hearts, are felt by the enemies of the country on every battle-field. What a glorious thought! thousands of the oppressed fighting for the redemption from slavery of a race which has ever worn the chain. When it is remembered that by this strife questions are to be settled which have ever disturbed the harmony of this country, and not that only, but questions which, when settled, will release millions of our fellow-men and women from the power of the oppressor, ought we not to be thankful that we are permitted to make great sacrifices in so good a cause?

CHAPTER IX.

The Seventh ordered to the East.—Expedition to Blue's Gap.—Skirmish on the Blooming pike.

After Floyd was driven from Cotton Hill, very few rebels remained in that portion of Virginia. Many troops were sent to Kentucky and elsewhere. Among the number was the Seventh Regiment. It was ordered to join the forces under command of General Kelley, which were operating on the upper waters of the Potomac, with headquarters at Cumberland, Maryland.

Accordingly, on the twelfth day of December, the regiment embarked on steamers, and after paying its respects to General Cox, by way of presenting arms and cheers, it moved down the river; thus leaving forever the scene of its past dangers and privations. Little had, apparently, been accomplished, during its summer campaign; but perils had been braved, privations had been suffered, and obstacles had been overcome. Many graves had been dug and filled with the pride of the regiment. These were left as a record of its patient suffering in that wild waste of hills. There was a sort of sadness attending the leaving of all this for a new field of operations. But the soldier's life is one continued change; and, therefore, he readily adapts himself to circumstances.

At Parkersburg the regiment left the boats, and took a train of cars, which conveyed it to Green Spring Run, a station on the Baltimore and Ohio Railroad, sixteen miles from Romney, Virginia. Here it remained without tents for several days, when it was ordered to Romney, to which place it proceeded immediately. It was now given a good ground for its camp, and furnished with Sibley tents, which were both warm and roomy. The weather being very fine for the time of year, the health and spirits of the soldiers rapidly improved.

During the occupation of Romney, quite a force of "bushwhackers" had collected at Blue's Gap, which were under command of Colonel Blue. This force of bandits had annoyed the Union citizens for some time. It was finally resolved to break it up. The force chosen to do this work consisted of the Fourth, Fifth, Seventh, and Eighth Ohio, Fourteenth Indiana, and First Virginia, with Danver's two companies of cavalry, and a section of Howard's Battery, in all about two thousand five hundred men, under command of Colonel Dunning of the Fifth Ohio. A little past midnight of January 6th, the force moved out from their camp. The night was bitter cold, but the march was rapid; and just after daybreak, the vicinity of the gap was reached, to find that the rebels were tearing up the flooring of the bridge leading over the stream coming through the gap. The skirmishers drove this force away, and then advanced over the bridge, followed by the Fifth Ohio, which took possession of Blue's house. Procuring a negro woman for a guide, the force advanced to assault the rebel stronghold on the mountain. On reaching the place, the intrenchments were handsomely carried, the rebels standing for five rounds only, when they broke, and fled down the side of the mountain. Their flight was so rapid that many of the fugitives ran on to the Fourth Ohio, which was at hand, and were captured. But they were hardly worth taking, for an uglier set of ragamuffins the mountains of Virginia, or the whole world even, could hardly produce. Blue's property was utterly destroyed. The loss of the enemy in this affair was forty killed, and as many taken prisoners, together with all their stores, wagons, and ammunition. A number of cattle were also taken and driven back to Romney. On their return, the Federals fired several houses, which was a lasting disgrace to all those taking part in it. General Kelley was justly indignant at this conduct.

Nothing further occurred to break the *ennui* of camp and picket duty until the 10th, when an order came to break camp and prepare for a march. Immediately following this order, all was bustle and confusion, in anticipation of an advance. There being a lack of transportation, some tents and commissary stores were burned. In early evening, the regiment marched into the town, where it was compelled to wait, through a fearful storm of sleet, until midnight, when, instead of an advance, the entire force rapidly fell back through Springfield to Patterson's Creek, on the Baltimore and Ohio Railroad. This camp was soon converted into a mud-hole. If all of Virginia had been canvassed a worse place for a camp could not have been found. After a few weeks contest with this everlasting snow and mud, an order came, on the 5th of February, to march, which was hailed with universal joy.

The force passed down the railroad late in the afternoon, for a short distance; when, leaving the tents and baggage, it took a road to the right, and before night halted in a grove by the roadside. After a few hours spent in preparing and eating supper, it moved off in the direction of Romney, the Seventh in the advance.

All night we marched, over mountains and streams, through snow and sleet. In the morning we came to a halt at an old tannery, and after remaining through the day, fell back four miles and bivouacked on the banks of the Little Cacapon River. Tired and wet, the soldiers lay down to rest on their bed of rails and straw, to gather strength for the morrow. At last, day dawned, rainy and gloomy, and the command moved five miles to the rear, to a place called the Levels,—a very high table-land, exposed to severe wind and storm, which never fails to visit that region. The regiment was ordered to bivouac, and soon the pine forest was converted into a village of green houses, with hot fires roaring and crackling before them.

We remained here some fifteen days, within three miles of the tents; but for some reason, better known to those in command, we were left on a hilltop, exposed to the cold winds and snows of February, in brush shanties. During some of the time it was so cold that a crust formed on the snow sufficiently hard to hold up a person. During this time the commanding officer of our brigade occupied a house close by, which was very convenient as well as comfortable.

The regiment, while here, did very little duty; in fact none, with the exception of one brigade drill in the snow, which only vexed the command, without accomplishing any good.

Colonel Sprague, formerly captain of Company E, now paid the regiment a visit, the first time he had met his old comrades since his capture. Following that had intervened his long imprisonment. The meeting was a pleasant one.

On the 13th of March the regiment left camp, and, taking the Bradford pike, crossed a range of hills, at the foot of which is the Baltimore and Ohio Railroad. Taking this road, Pau-Pau Station was reached before night. Here we found quite a number of troops.

General Lander advanced with one brigade on the Blooming pike. Soon the advance-guard, consisting of a part of a regiment of cavalry, came on to an intrenched camp of militia. The general, taking command in person, ordered a charge; but barely a dozen of these horsemen could be made to follow their brave leader. But, nothing daunted, Lander, followed by his staff and a few of the cavalry, dashed over the intrenchments, when some fifty rebels surrendered; Colonel Baldwin, their commander, giving himself up to Lander, after the latter had seized him by the shoulder, despite the revolver which the rebel colonel held in his hand.

On the return of this expedition, the Seventh was ordered out on to the pike. After advancing for nearly two miles, it halted by the roadside, where it remained in the mud and snow till the following afternoon, when it went into camp close by.

CHAPTER X.

Gallantry of Lieutenant O'Brien.—Death of General Lander.—The Seventh escort his remains.—The occupation of Winchester.

During the occupation of the country about Pau-Pau Station, the troops were kept active. Skirmishes were of frequent occurrence. One of them is deserving of mention. A reconnoissance was being made by Lieutenant O'Brien, of Lander's staff, accompanied by twenty or more cavalry, when they were met by a band of rebels, who immediately fired a volley; following which, they demanded the small party of Federals to surrender. O'Brien, riding to the front, declined, at the same time emptying the saddle of the foremost rebel with a revolver, which he had in his hand ready for use. The lieutenant soon after received a fatal wound in the shoulder, from the effects of which he died some weeks after. Seeing their leader disabled, the Union cavalry hurried him to the rear, at the same time presenting a determined front. When he had arrived at a safe distance they fell back, fighting as they went. They thus brought the gallant O'Brien safe to headquarters.

O'Brien was a writer of some note. Before the war he was a contributor to several periodicals, among which was the Atlantic Monthly. For these magazines he wrote many elegant things, which their readers will probably remember.

On the first day of March, the monotony of life in camp was broken by an order to march. We moved out of camp, followed by the entire division, on the road leading to Winchester. Towards evening we crossed the Big Cacapon River, and after ascending a spur of the Shenandoah Mountain, filed into a grove of pines, and remained till the following afternoon, when an order was given to fall back. On returning to our camp, we found that the retrograde movement was occasioned by the sudden death of General Lander. The brave soldier and able commander expired while his troops were moving on an important position of the enemy,—a campaign which his fertile brain had conceived, and which his daring and dash were to put into successful execution. No wonder, then, when the spirit of its leader took its flight, that the division was recalled. None were found competent to succeed him in the command of an expedition which had occupied his every thought while he had been connected with the department.

On Monday, March 3d, the Seventh regiment escorted his remains to the cars, in the presence of fifteen thousand troops, drawn up in line to pay their respects, for the last time, to all that was left of a commander whom they loved, and a soldier whom they admired. This slow, sad march of the Seventh, to the strains of a solemn dirge, was impressive. We returned to camp with the reflection that a master spirit had taken its departure.

After the death of General Lander, Brigadier-General Shields was given the command of his division. He arrived soon after.

The forces under General Banks, occupying the country in the vicinity of Harper's Ferry, were ordered to make an immediate advance on Winchester, General Shields was directed to co-operate in this movement. He was ordered to move on Martinsburg, when General Banks crossed the Potomac.

Early in March the division moved down to the railroad, when on the same day it took the cars for Martinsburg. On arriving at Back Creek, ten miles east of Hancock, the bridge was found to be destroyed. The command now bivouacked, while a party was set at work repairing the bridge. The work progressed so slowly, that on the 10th the command moved on in advance of the train, passing through Martinsburg, and encamping some two miles out on the Winchester pike.

On the following morning the column pushed vigorously forward to assist General Banks in his attack on Winchester. The rebels, however, instead of giving battle, fled as the command approached the city. Shields, therefore, was ordered to encamp his troops before reaching Winchester. The camp of the Seventh was about three miles north of the town, on the Martinsburg road. The balance of the division encamped in the immediate vicinity.

Winchester had for a long time been occupied by the rebels. The extreme left of Beauregard's army, under command of General Johnston, had taken possession of the place, when the rebel troops first occupied Virginia. From this point, troops were immediately sent forward to occupy and destroy the Baltimore and Ohio Railroad, as well as to menace our lines in the direction of Harper's Ferry and Cumberland. The possession, therefore, of the place by the Union forces was of great importance. It not only resulted in the protection of this very important railroad, but so menaced the left of the rebel army as to require its commander to detach a large force to the Shenandoah Valley, and thus materially weakening his main army. Under a leader less able than Jackson, it would have greatly taxed his energies to hold the valley. But under this indomitable general the army was enabled to make a good show of resistance to the advance of the Federal forces.

Winchester, the county seat of Frederick County, is seventy-four miles west of Washington. The town is laid out in regular order, the streets crossing at right angles. The place possesses some little of historical interest. During the French and Indian War, Washington made it his headquarters; and he also mentions it as one of the points which he touched while on his mission to the French authorities on the Ohio River. After the engagement at Great Meadows, July 4, 1774, Washington returned to the place to recruit his regiment. It was also the base of operations for the forces engaged in the reduction of Fort Duquesne. During these wars a fort was built under the direction of Washington, and named Fort Landon. A part of it is to be seen at this day. While this fort was being constructed, Washington bought a lot in Winchester, had a blacksmith shop built on it, and brought his own smith from Mount Vernon to do the necessary iron-work for the fort. A well was sunk in this fort to the depth of one hundred and three feet, the water from which now runs over the top. The labor of erecting this fort was performed by Washington's own regiment. The famous General Morgan, the leader of the American forces at the battle of the Cowpens, is buried here.

CHAPTER XI.

A Reconnoissance to Strasburg. — Battle of Winchester. — Utter defeat and rout of Jackson's army.

Immediately after the occupation of Winchester, the enemy's cavalry advance becoming troublesome, a plan was laid for its capture. Colonel Mason, of the Fourth Ohio, was sent out on the road to Front Royal, with a brigade, composed of infantry, cavalry, and artillery, with instructions to proceed until he arrived at the last road leading to the right before reaching Front Royal; which road he was to take, and by it strike the rear of the enemy at Middletown, a small hamlet equally distant from both Winchester and Strasburg. He was soon after followed by General Shields, with six thousand men, who moved on the direct road to Middletown. Colonel Mason's command, arriving at this place in advance of Shields' column, encountered the enemy's pickets, and drove them to Cedar Creek Bridge, which, having covered with combustibles, they fired. When the troops of Colonel Mason arrived in the vicinity, they were opened upon by a battery, to which they replied; with no effect, however, as the distance was too great. Shields coming up with his division soon after, the entire force bivouacked for the night.

Early the following morning the command crossed the river without opposition; but on arriving at Strasburg, the enemy opened fire from a battery planted on a hill beyond the town. Shields, suspecting that the entire force of Jackson was in the vicinity, made his dispositions for immediate battle. The Seventh being ordered out on the road beyond the town, were fired upon by a masked battery, but none injured. After having been exposed to this fire for half an hour, it was withdrawn. Soon after, our artillery was got into position, and after thirty pieces of cannon had belched forth their fire, the rebels fled in haste. During this fire, Mason's cavalry advanced so far out on the road, that they were mistaken for the enemy by Captain Clark, of a battery of regulars; he therefore sent a shell among them, with such accuracy as to kill a few horses, and slightly wound one man.

An advance being ordered, the pursuit was continued for five miles, when the command returned to Strasburg, and encamped for the night. On the following morning it fell back to its old camp, the Seventh marching twenty-two miles in seven hours, with but one halt.

This reconnoissance to Strasburg leaving no doubt on the minds of both Banks and Shields that the enemy was not in the front in force, the first division of Banks's corps, on the 20th, commenced its movement to Manassas, in accordance with a letter of instruction from General McClellan, of the 16th. General Banks did not follow this division immediately, but remained at Winchester until twelve o'clock on Sunday, the 23d, when he started for Harper's Ferry.

All this time Shields thought he was being trifled with by the rebel General Ashby.

On Saturday, the 22d, there had been a good deal of firing in the early part of the day, but what occasioned it did not seem to be well understood, except to those engaged. But during the afternoon it was thought prudent to make all needful preparation for battle, so as not to be surprised in case it should prove that a greater force than Ashby's was in front. Therefore the whole division was ordered up; the third brigade, however, did not pass through the town. Shields went to the front, followed by the first and second brigades. As these forces emerged from the city, the rebel cavalry made a dash at the pickets, who fled in some confusion through the little hamlet of Kernstown, but rallied soon after, and by a well-directed volley of musketry emptied several rebel saddles. This success enabled them to retire in safety. The rebel cavalry soon after advanced, when a sharp skirmish ensued. Our pickets having been re-enforced by several detached companies, were enabled to maintain their ground. In the mean time the rebels opened on our lines from a battery planted on an eminence; immediately after which a Union battery wheeled into position, when a spirited artillery duel took place. While directing the fire of this battery, Shields was struck on the arm by a fragment of a shell, fracturing the arm, and producing a painful wound. He, however, continued in the field for some time after the accident occurred, but was finally taken to a house close by, and his arm dressed, after which he was taken to town in an ambulance.

The firing having ceased, the first brigade went into camp on the spot, while the second brigade encamped in the rear. The third brigade filed into an open field near where they were stationed during the operations in front.

During Saturday night a strong picket was kept well out to the front, while the remaining troops slept on their arms. Nothing occurred during the night to disturb the several camps.

Morning dawned bright and pleasant. The stillness which rested over the field of the previous day's operations, gave token of the intention of the belligerents to respect the Sabbath-day. In view of the general quiet, the second and third brigades were ordered back to their camp on the Martinsburg pike.

It was nearly noon when the Seventh arrived, and before the men had barely time to eat a hurriedly prepared dinner, it was again ordered forward. This time the march was rapid. The distant booming of cannon, induced many a disturbed reflection as to what lay before us. As we passed through Winchester to the south, we emerged into an open plain. This was crowded with people, as were also the house-tops. They had assembled, apparently, for the purpose of seeing the Union army defeated and crushed, and to welcome the victors into the city.

Arriving on the field, we found our forces occupying a commanding position in rear of a range of hills overlooking Kernstown; while the batteries, posted at intervals on the crest of these hills, were maintaining a heavy fire on the right of the enemy's position, which alone seemed to give evidence of any purpose to advance. The left of our line was held by the Second brigade, Colonel Sullivan; while the centre and right were held by the First brigade. Colonel Kimball, commanding the division, was stationed on a commanding eminence, from which several batteries were pouring their shot and shell into the enemy whenever he showed himself within range.

Up to this time, the main fighting had occurred in front of our left; but soon after a battery opened in front of the right, from a piece of timber, which our batteries were unable to silence. It became evident, from this, that the heavy skirmishing which the enemy had kept up from their right was simply a feint, for the purpose of drawing the greater part of our force to that part of the field, when a spirited onslaught would be made on the other flank, which was expected to turn our right wing, and thus give them the victory. It was a conception worthy the genius of a Jackson, but it was entirely unsuccessful, as no troops were sent to that part of the field beyond what ordinary prudence required; but on the contrary, becoming satisfied of the intention of the enemy, Colonel Kimball resolved to charge this battery. The work was assigned to the Third brigade. Colonel Tyler, calling in the Seventh, which had been supporting a battery from the time it arrived on the field, formed his brigade in column, by divisions, and immediately moved forward; at the same time changing direction to the right, and passing up a ravine, shielded by a piece of timber which skirted it on the side towards the enemy.

After arriving at some distance to the right, the column changed direction to the left; and after a march of nearly a mile, it arrived on the flank, and partly in the rear of the enemy. It had now reached an eminence in a dense wood. In front, the battery which was the object of our movement was playing vigorously upon the First brigade, to which a spirited fire was returned by Robinson's Battery, which had wheeled into position on the extreme right. This acted as a cover to the movements of our brigade. Breathless, and with anxious hearts, we awaited the return of our scouts, which would be the signal for a plunge into the unknown. We were not kept long in suspense, for in a few minutes the order was given to change direction to the left, and the column moved forward, preceded by a line of skirmishers. After marching in silence for some distance, the sharpshooters opened a destructive fire on us from behind trees. We were immediately ordered to charge; and, with a prolonged yell, the command, led by the Seventh Ohio, swept like a torrent down the hill. A ravine now lay in front, and, at a short distance, a slight eminence, and still beyond, a solid stone wall, behind which, in three lines, nine regiments of the enemy lay concealed. It was a fearful moment. The rebel artillery, in the rear of this stone wall, had been turned upon the advancing column. The grape and canister was tearing the bark from the trees over our heads, while the solid shot and shell made great gaps in their trunks. Under our feet the turf was being torn up, and around and about us the air was thick with flying missiles. Not a gun was fired on our side. The head of the column soon reached the ravine, when a deafening discharge of musketry greeted us. A sheet of flame shot along the stone wall, followed by an explosion that shook the earth, and the missiles tore through the solid ranks of the command with a fearful certainty. The brigade staggered—halted. With breathless anxiety we anticipated a counter-charge by the rebels; but it came not. Victory to our arms followed that omission on the part of the enemy. The order being given to fire, the column recovered from the confusion into which it had been temporarily thrown. The Seventh now advanced to the eminence beyond the ravine; and, from a partial cover, maintained the unequal contest till the other regiments could form and come to its support. The One Hundred and Tenth Pennsylvania Regiment was thrown into such confusion, that it was of little service during the remainder of the day.

An order was given to the Seventh to prolong its line to the left. An attempt was made to execute the order, when the left wing, passing over a fence into an open field, received such a well-directed fire as to compel it to fall back to its old position.

During this part of the contest, the rebels endeavored to extend their left, so as to flank us on the right. To meet this movement, Tyler ordered the First Virginia to move to the right. Passing into an open field, it was exposed to a cross-fire, which soon drove it back to the timber.

The roar of musketry was now deafening. The dying and the dead were lying thick upon the hillside, but neither army seemed to waver. The confusion attending the getting of troops into action had ceased. The great "dance of death" seemed to be going forward without a motion. The only evidence of life on that gory field, was the vomiting forth of flame and smoke from thousands of well-aimed muskets. From that blue column, which rolled and tumbled in its ascent from the battle-field, the unerring bullet sped on its errand of death. But other regiments are seen coming to the rescue. The right wing of the gallant Eighth Ohio takes position on the left, followed by the no less gallant Thirteenth and Fourteenth Indiana, Fifth and Sixty-seventh Ohio, and Eighty-fourth Pennsylvania. These regiments opened a heavy fire, which was replied to by the enemy in gallant style.

The battle now raged fiercely until near night, when the enemy began to show signs of giving way. At this the Union forces advanced a little, at the same time delivering their fire with accuracy. As the shades of evening deepened into night, the enemy began to fall back. At this crisis, Colonel Kimball ordered a charge along the whole line, when the retreat became a rout. In their flight, the enemy left in front of the Third brigade two pieces of artillery and four caissons.

That night the Seventh bivouacked on the spot now made historic by its gallantry. The wounded were being brought in all night long, while the dead were lying in heaps around us, their increasing distortions and ghastliness adding new horrors to the battle-field.

At early dawn the next day, we were ready to renew the work of blood and carnage; but there was no occasion; the victory of the day before was complete, the rebels had no desire of renewing the contest. They gave the advancing column a few parting salutes from a battery, and then beat a hasty retreat. We followed them that day to Cedar Run, where just at night a slight skirmish occurred, with some loss to the rebels. The following day the Union forces occupied Strasburg, when the pursuit ceased.

CHAPTER XII.

General Shields' anxiety for laurels.—Summing up of the battle.—Losses in the Seventh.

After the battle of Winchester, General Shields showed a disposition to appropriate the laurels won by others to himself. In a letter to a friend at Washington, he claimed that, after the reconnoissance to Strasburg, on the 18th, he fell back hurriedly, for the purpose of deceiving the enemy into the belief that his force was small; and that after arriving at Winchester, he moved his division beyond the town, so as to create the belief in the minds of the citizens that most of his force had been sent away. Now the fact is, this reconnoissance was greatly the result of accident. The original design of it was to capture the enemy's advance; this failing, the force proceeded to Strasburg for the purpose of discovering whether or not the enemy was in force in the vicinity. It was clearly shown by this advance, what was afterwards well known, that nothing but a small cavalry force occupied Strasburg, and that Jackson was some distance up the valley. The hurried march of the division back to Winchester, was also the result of accident. The command marched left in front, which brought a regiment in the advance whose colonel cared little for the comfort of his men; hence the rapid march. Shields reached Winchester in advance of the command, having gone on before. After our return there was no change of position, as our tents had not been disturbed, and we reoccupied them as they were before leaving. If Jackson was deceived, the credit of it is not due to Shields, for he was confident to the very last that there was no other force in his front than Ashby. Even as late as Sunday noon, when in reality the battle had begun, he ridiculed the idea of Colonel Kimball calling for so many troops, remarking, that "Kimball wanted more troops than was necessary for the force in front of him." He also boastfully said, that "Jackson knew him, and was afraid of him."

His friends tried to make it appear that it was by his direction that the troops were manœuvred on the field of battle. Now the fact is, he was four miles away, and in such a condition from a wound that he compelled one of the best surgeons of the division to remain with him till long after the battle, against the request of the medical director, who represented to him, in the most earnest manner, that the wounded were suffering for the want of medical attention. In thus retaining a surgeon for his own purpose, while the wounded were suffering for medical aid, he was criminal in the extreme. He committed an offence which ought to have deprived him of his commission.

Colonel Kimball was mainly instrumental in achieving the victory, assisted, of course, by those under his command. The skilful manner, however, in which the troops were managed was entirely due to him; and the authorities regarded it in that light, for he was immediately made a brigadier-general, as were both Tyler and Sullivan.

The number of rebel forces engaged in the battle of Winchester has been variously estimated. They probably numbered sixteen regiments of infantry, four full batteries of artillery, together with one of four guns; in the aggregate, twenty-eight pieces and three battalions of cavalry, under Ashby and Stewart;—in all, eleven thousand men. The Union forces consisted of thirteen regiments of infantry, four full batteries of artillery and a section; in the aggregate, twenty-six pieces, and a battalion of cavalry;—in all, nine thousand men.

The rebel army was the attacking force, yet the engagement between the infantry was on ground of their own choosing, by reason of the Third brigade charging one of their batteries. It was in the vicinity of this battery, which was at least a mile in advance of our selected line of battle, that the fighting occurred which turned the tide of battle. At this point the enemy had every advantage of position. He was securely posted behind a stone wall, and in a belt of timber extending along a ridge; while our forces were compelled to advance across a plain exposed to a galling fire from infantry and artillery; and it was not until they arrived within eighty yards of his line that any thing like a fair ground could be obtained. Jackson, the famous commander of the no-less famous "stone-wall brigade," a sobriquet it had obtained at Bull Run, was fairly beaten; and that, too, by a force without a general, and of inferior numbers. The victory was so complete, that the enemy left two hundred and twenty-five dead on the field. Their killed and wounded amounted to nearly nine hundred, while their loss in prisoners was upwards of two hundred and fifty: adding stragglers and deserters to these figures, and it will swell the number to about two thousand. The Fifth Virginia rebel regiment was nearly annihilated: there was hardly sufficient of it left to preserve its organization.

The loss to the Seventh was fourteen killed and fifty-one wounded: but few were taken prisoners, and those by accident. The following is the list:

Killed.—Orderly-Sergeant A. C. Danforth; Corporal A. C. Griswold; privates, Charles Stern, James Carroll, James Creiglow, Allen C. Lamb, Stephen W. Rice, E. G. Sackett, Reuben Burnham, Louis Carven, Elias Hall, John Fram, Fred. Groth, James Bish.

Wounded.—Captain J. F. Asper; Lieutenant Samuel McClelland; Sergeant-Major J. P. Webb, and Sergeant A. J. Kelly, mortally; sergeants, A. H. Fitch, E. M. Lazonny; corporals, Ed. Kelley, William Saddler, Geo. Blandin, William E. Smith, Benjamin Gridley; privates, Fred. Hoffman, Daniel Clancey, Leander Campbell, Joseph Miller, Hampton Gardner, Arthur Lappin, Thomas Fresher, Duncan Reid, Joseph Smith, Albert E. Withers, Charles Fagan, O. H. Worcester, W. Coleman, Stephen Kellogg, John Gardner, F. M. Palmer, F. A. Warner, Daniel Kingsbury, Richard Winsor, John Milliman, John Atwater, Geo. Anness, Fred. Bethel, Charles W. Minnick, Moses Owens, Arba Pritchell, Edward Thompson, Edward E. Tracy, A. A. Cavanaha, S. Bishop, Owen Gregory, James Hunt, W. McClurg, H. M. McQuiston, D. O'Conner, P. Tenny, Richard Phillips, T. B. Danon, Wm. Birch, Henry Clemens.

CHAPTER XIII.

Pursuit of Jackson up the Valley.—March to Fredericksburg, and return to Front Royal.

About the 1st of April the command left Strasburg, under command of General Banks, driving the rear-guard of the enemy through the little village of Woodstock, and taking a position on the banks of Stoney Creek, four miles beyond the latter place. It remained here until the 17th, during which time the enemy kept up an artillery fire across the creek, which resulted in the killing of several men in the division of General Williams.

On the morning of the 17th the command crossed the creek, and stormed the enemy's battery on the opposite shore. The early dawn was brightening up the eastern horizon with tints of red; and, as the command emerged from the bridge, and ascended the steep hill beyond, their bayonets glistened and sparkled. After firing one volley, the rebels fled in haste, leaving the Federal forces to advance without opposition. After falling back beyond the north branch of the Shenandoah River, they made a stand, and endeavored to burn the bridge, but were prevented by the Union cavalry. A flank movement being ordered, and partly executed, the rebels again abandoned their position. The Federals now pressed on to within a short distance of New Market, where they encamped.

Here the command remained ten days, when it moved two miles south of the town, and on the 3d of May advanced to within a few miles of Harrisonburg, but on the following day fell back about five miles to a good defensive position.

The tents were now ordered to be turned over to the quartermaster; and on the following Monday we wound our way through Brook's Gap, in the Massanutten Mountains, towards the smoky tops of the Blue Ridge, and thus leaving forever the beautiful valley of the north branch of the Shenandoah. Towards evening we crossed the south branch of the same river at Columbia Bridge, and moved on in the direction of Luray, encamping near that place. The next morning the command moved on down the river until night, when it encamped. In the evening a hard rain storm came up, which continued for several days. In early evening of the following day the command reached Front Royal, a small village situated at the base of the Blue Ridge, near the junction of the two branches of the Shenandoah River. The following morning we crossed the Blue Ridge, and immediately encountered the enemy's cavalry, which annoyed us for several days. On the 17th we arrived at Warrenton, a delightful village in Fauquier County. We remained in this camp until Monday morning, when we again took the line of march for Fredericksburg. We reached Falmouth, on the north bank of the Rappahannock River, on the 23d of May. The corps of McDowell was in the immediate vicinity, numbering thirty thousand men, and one hundred pieces of artillery.

When we arrived on the Rappahannock, we learned that this force of McDowell's, now numbering forty-one thousand men, was ordered down to Richmond, to form a junction with the right wing of the grand army under McClellan. There were then only about twelve thousand of the enemy in front of

Fredericksburg. It was about fifty miles to the extreme right of the army in front of Richmond.

On Saturday the President and secretary of war came down for the purpose of arranging the details. Shields' division was greatly in need of shoes and clothing, while the ammunition for the artillery had been condemned, and another supply, which had been ordered, had been very much delayed. It was therefore arranged that the force should start early on Monday morning, both the President and McDowell being averse to starting on Sunday.

That evening the President and secretary of war left for Washington. Very soon after, General McDowell received a telegram, to the effect that Jackson was making a raid down the Shenandoah Valley, with a prospect of crushing the forces under General Banks. Soon after this dispatch, another arrived from the secretary of war, by order of the President, containing instructions to send a division after Jackson. Here was the fatal blow to the campaign against Richmond. McDowell promptly ordered General Shields' division to move, and at the same time telegraphed the President that it was a fatal blow to them all.

Little things control momentous events. Jackson's army of twenty thousand veterans checkmated an army of one hundred and fifty thousand men. In defending Washington, we lost Richmond; but Jackson risked his own communication to break ours. Results more than realized his expectations. Without risk there is little gain. Jackson adopted this adage into his tactics, and endangered his army to save it. Events proved his sagacity.

In time of war the capital of a country, unless far removed from the seat of war, is in the way. The City of Washington was a fatality. It stood between the army and victory. Jackson knew this, and profited by it. When this general menaced Washington, our army let go its hold on the Confederacy, to make it doubly safe. The campaign against Richmond was abandoned, but Washington was endangered still. The valleys and swamps of the Chickahominy were paved with the bodies of heroes—the little rivulets were swollen with the best blood of the land—an army of cripples were given to charity;—and for what? That the City of Washington might be safe. We have since then fought the ground over again from Washington to Richmond; another graveyard has been planted; and this time for a purpose. Washington has been set aside by the new commander, and Richmond made the objective point.

CHAPTER XIV.

The march on Waynesboro'.—Two brigades encounter Jackson at Port Republic, and after five hours' fighting are compelled to fall back.

Nearly the entire corps of General McDowell followed the division of General Shields. The latter took the direction of Manassas Junction, and from there passed down the railroad, through Manassas Gap, arriving at Front Royal on Friday noon, after a sharp engagement with a small force of rebels.

Soon after, Shields stationed one brigade on the Luray road, another to watch the fords of the Shenandoah, another was sent out on the Strasburg road, while the remaining one occupied the town. On McDowell's arrival, Shields, with his entire division, was ordered out on the road to Strasburg, for the purpose of intercepting the retreat of the enemy. But, instead of taking the road which he was ordered to take, he crossed over the north branch of the Shenandoah River on the road to Winchester. It then being too late to repair the mischief, and get ahead of Jackson, Shields was permitted to go in the direction of Luray, and follow up Jackson as far as he thought advisable, with the single instruction, that, in no event, should his division be separated; so that each brigade would be in supporting distance of all the others.

On the second day we arrived in the vicinity of Columbia Bridge, and pitched our tents for the purpose, as we supposed, of enjoying a night's rest; but towards evening an order was received to fall back six miles. Arriving at this new camp, we again pitched our tents; but just at dark we received an order to move forward to the camp we had but just left. We arrived about midnight, and slept on the ground; thus wasting the strength of the command in a needless march of twelve miles.

On the following morning, June 7th, the Third brigade, by an order to move on Waynesboro', took up the line of march, arriving in early evening on the banks of Naked Creek, where it went into camp. Colonel Carroll's Second brigade had passed over the road some time before.

The command had nothing but flour and beef for supper, and nothing for breakfast on the following morning; but being assured that some hard bread was in waiting, some six miles ahead, it cheerfully pressed forward at four o'clock A.M., and at about two o'clock the same day, reached the vicinity of Port Republic, where Colonel Carroll's brigade had met with a repulse the day before.

Port Republic is situated at the junction of two forks of the south branch of the Shenandoah River. Jackson's whole army was in the vicinity of the place, the most of it occupying the west bank of the river. In rear of Jackson's position, at Cross Keys, were General Fremont's forces. At the latter place, on the previous day, Fremont had defeated Jackson, with heavy loss to the latter.

Jackson having thus failed to beat back Fremont, was compelled to cross the river at Port Republic, and, defeating Shields' command, pass through a gap in the mountain to Gordonsville.

When General Tyler's command arrived on the field, Lieutenant-Colonel Daum, chief of artillery, advised an immediate attack; but the general wisely concluded to await the order of General Shields. Selecting a good position for defence, the command bivouacked for the night.

Early in the morning of June 9th, the enemy was seen to debouch into the plain in our front, when our artillery, under Captains Clark, Robinson, and Huntington, opened a heavy fire upon him. This force moved into the woods on our left, and passing up a spur of the Blue Ridge, threw themselves rapidly forward, with a view of turning that wing of the army. Two companies of skirmishers and two regiments of infantry were sent into the woods to counteract this movement. The skirmishers having become warmly engaged, two more regiments were sent forward to their support. The enemy now abandoned his intention, and coming out of the woods, swept across the field to our right, uniting with a column which was advancing to the attack.

During this time, the Seventh was supporting a section of Huntington's Battery. This new movement was directed against the position occupied by it. When arriving within range of the guns, the enemy charged. The regiment reserved its fire until the rebel column approached within easy range, when, by order of Colonel Creighton, the regiment, which had hitherto been concealed by the tall spires of wheat, rose to its feet, and delivered its fire. This shower of lead made a fearful gap in the lines of the advancing column. It staggered, and finally halted. The Seventh now plunged into the midst of the foe, when an awful scene of carnage followed. After a short struggle, the enemy was pressed back, followed by the exultant victors. The Fifth and Twenty-ninth Ohio regiments did gallant service in this charge. When the enemy had been pressed back for half a mile, the column halted, reformed, and then fell back to its old position.

The enemy now made a furious attack on the extreme right of the division, to meet which the Seventh changed front on the Fourth company. The enemy was soon driven back in great confusion, and with heavy loss. Immediately recovering from this temporary check, he made an onslaught on the centre, which resulted in his repulse, with greater loss than in any previous attack; the Fifth Ohio alone capturing a piece of artillery and many prisoners.

During these operations, the enemy sent a heavy column against our left; and debouching from the timber, came down with such rapidity as to overwhelm the small force of infantry supporting four guns of Clark's Battery. This force, endeavoring to make a defence, came near being captured. The guns, of course, fell into the hands of the enemy. The Seventh and Fifth Ohio regiments were now directed to regain the position. Moving by the left flank to the rear of the position under a heavy fire, these two regiments dashed up the hill and over the guns, into the midst of the terrified rebels. Five color-bearers had now been shot down, while advancing as many rods. Lieutenant King seized the colors and pressed forward, followed by the regiment, which sent volley after volley after the fugitives, the firing ceasing only when the rebels were covered by a friendly hill. We were soon ordered to drive them from this position, which was done in gallant style, the command charging up the steep sides of the hill, in the face of the foe.

A large column of the enemy was now seen advancing from the bridge to the scene of action. It was therefore thought advisable by General Tyler to withdraw from the field during this check of the enemy, and before these re-enforcements could be brought into the contest.

This movement was executed under the direction of Colonel Carroll; and, with few exceptions, the retreat was as orderly as the advance.

After falling back some miles, we met the balance of the command under General Shields, who assumed the direction of the forces. Eighteen miles from the battle-field, the command halted for the night; and, on the third day, reached the vicinity of Luray, where it went into camp.

The importance of this engagement has been underrated. Great and beneficial results to the Union army would have followed a victory; as it was, a great disaster succeeded. The impetuous Jackson having thus prevented McDowell's forces from uniting with the grand army, dashed down in front of Richmond, and hurling his army against the right wing of McClellan, gave the Federal army its first check, which finally resulted in its overthrow. McClellan expecting McDowell, received Jackson. Had the former formed a junction with him, the grand army would have entered Richmond; but receiving Jackson, it entered Washington. This failure to intercept Jackson was due to General Shields' disobedience of orders. His entire division should have been on the ground on Sunday, or none of it; and on its arrival, he should have burned the bridge: then the capture of Jackson would have been rendered probable, but, as events occurred, it was impossible. A part of the division not being in supporting distance, rendered the burning of the bridge a necessity; but Shields regarded it differently. His order to save the bridge was the extreme of folly. To make himself a name, he came near sacrificing his command. On Sunday, Colonel Carroll's forces were in a position to have burned the bridge. Soon after, the enemy commanded it, with eighteen pieces of cannon. Early in the day it was safe to approach it—afterwards, madness.

This bridge in his possession, gave the enemy an opportunity to debouch on to the open plain. When there, the advance of Shields' division was liable to be crushed. The preservation of the bridge rendered it certain that he would be there, because this plain lay between him and safety. To avoid entering it, was to surrender. The shrewd Jackson chose to enter it. When there, he turned upon Tyler, and overwhelmed him; then moved off at his leisure. The defeat of Tyler was certain; his escape, marvellous. Jackson anticipated an easy victory, but met with a stubborn resistance. This mistake of Jackson saved Tyler.

When McDowell saw that the pursuit of Jackson was a failure, he endeavored to collect his forces at Fredericksburg, for the purpose of carrying out his original intention of joining McClellan; but Jackson was there before him, and the grand army had been beaten back.

Had the forces of Generals Banks and Fremont been left to take care of Jackson, and thus left McDowell with his 41,000 men free to go down to Richmond, the labor of historians would have been lessened.

Soon after the battle of Port Republic, General Shields was relieved of his command. This order received the approbation of both officers and men.

The following is a list of killed and wounded:

Killed.—Sergeant William Voges; corporals, Geo. R. Magary, Julius Ruoff, L. R. Gates, John H. Woodward; privates, Adolf Snyder, Romaine J. Kingsbury, John Mulligan, John Reber.

Wounded.—Captain Geo. L. Wood; First-lieutenant A. H. Day; sergeants, Virgil E. Smalley, Samuel Whaler, James R. Loucks (mortally), Chas. L. King, Wm. Lanterwasser (mortally); corporals, Townley Gillett (mortally), Holland B. Fry, Mark V. Burt, A. C. Lovett, Cyrus H. DeLong, A. C. Trimmer, Charles Knox;

privates, J. H. Burton, S. E. Buchanan, Isaac Maxfield, Charles Keller, F. Keller, Edwin B. Atwater, M. N. Hamilton (mortally), Daniel S. Judson (mortally), Wm. H. Pelton, Benjamin F. Hawkins, Lawson Hibbard, James L. Vancise, John Atwater, Jay Haskins, Leroy Chapman, Sylvester B. Matthews, Alfred W. Morley, Lawrence Remmel, George K. Carl, Franklin Eldridge, George Geyelin, John T. Geary, Ira Herrick, Marion Hoover, W. W. Rogers (mortally), Edwin Woods, Morris Osborn, G. W. Parker, M. Eckenrode, D. L. Hunt, William Frasher, Anthony Williams, John Smith, James Decker, Michael Campbell, Philip Anthony, John Colburn, John Hummel, John Luetke, John Schoembs, Conrad Sommer, John Voelker, Herman Fetzer.

CHAPTER XV.

Battle of Cedar Mountain.—Gallantry of the regiment, and terrible loss.

After a few days' rest at Luray, the regiment marched to Front Royal, and soon after left for Alexandria, where it arrived on the 27th of June. It went into camp on a beautiful hill, just outside the fortifications.

Remaining in this camp for a month, the regiment was ordered to join the forces under McDowell, at Warrenton. It arrived there on the morning of June 26th, and soon after reported to General Banks, at Little Washington.

General Tyler had now been relieved from duty with the Third brigade, and General Geary placed in command.

As early as the 16th of July, the advance of Jackson's forces was at Gordonsville; and by the 1st of August reached the vicinity of the Rapidan River. To meet this movement, General Pope, commanding the Army of Virginia, ordered forward the corps of General Banks; and on the 8th of August ordered General Sigel's corps to Culpepper to co-operate with Banks' forces; but Sigel, instead of moving promptly forward, sent a courier to know what road he should take, when in fact there was but one. This delayed the movement of his corps for several hours, so that it was impossible to get it in position in time to render any assistance to the forces under Banks.

On the 7th day of August, Crawford's brigade, of Banks' corps, had been pushed forward in the direction of Slaughter Mountain, to support General Bayard, whose brigade of cavalry was being driven back in that direction by the enemy; and on the 9th, to support this movement of Crawford, Banks was directed to take up a strong position a short distance in his rear. Rickett's division, of McDowell's corps, was posted three miles in rear of Banks' position, and within easy supporting distance.

Desultory artillery firing was kept up all day on the 9th; yet General Banks, apparently, did not think the enemy were in force, for, during the afternoon, he left the strong position which he had taken, by order of General Pope, and advanced to assault the enemy, believing that he could crush his advance before the main body came up.

The enemy was strongly posted, and sheltered by woods and ridges; while Banks had to pass over an open field, which was swept by the fire of the enemy thus concealed.

The intention of Jackson, in this advance, was to crush a detachment of Pope's army before the balance could come to its support. Banks, in thus advancing to the assault, aided him in his design, which otherwise would have been an entire failure.

Cedar Mountain, the position occupied by Jackson, is thus described: "The mountain is one of remarkable beauty. At a distance of four or five miles from its base it seems to rise like a perfect cone from the plain below, and from its base to its summit scarcely a deflection is to be observed in its outline form—a perfectly straight line, as if nature had formed it in the same manner that school-boys form sand-hills. The sides of the mountain are covered with a heavy growth of timber: its summit is reached by a poor road. The height of the summit is, perhaps, eight hundred feet above Cedar Creek."

Early in the day of the 9th, General Geary's brigade was sent to hold Telegraph Hill, from which our signal-officers had been driven. To approach this hill was sure slaughter; but the veteran brigade moved on, through a storm of shot and shell, and occupied the position.

Thirty pieces of cannon on our side, and as many on the side of the enemy, were belching forth their fire. There was no part of the Federal lines but that was swept by this fire.

A little after three o'clock the Seventh Regiment was ordered over the crest of the hill, into a cornfield beyond. While advancing to this position, a most terrific cannonade was directed against it. It seemed as if every cannon was being directed against this band of heroes; but it never faltered in this march of death, moving coolly on, regardless of the missiles that were tearing through its bleeding ranks. Comrades were falling, and brothers dying; the mangled, bleeding victims of the fury and violence of war were left thick, making the ground sacred on which they fell; but the line wavered not. Reaching a low place, the regiment halted, and the boys threw themselves upon the ground; and thus for a long hour they lay, in an open field, exposed to a hot sun, with a hail-storm of grape, canister, and shell falling thick and fast around them. Men gave up their lives so gently, that it was almost impossible to tell the living from the dead. The fatal missile struck its victim, leaving the lifeless clay in the same attitude which the living body but just before occupied. During that fatal period death assumed a real character, while life seemed but a dream.

The engagement had now become general. The brigade of General Prince had advanced on the left of Geary, occupying the prolongation of the line. Artillery replied to artillery, musketry to musketry, bayonet to bayonet, in this deadly strife. Daring warmed into rashness, and bravery into recklessness.

About four o'clock the regiment was ordered into a meadow, which position it promptly occupied, although the fire had not slackened, and carnage marked its advance. After dressing the lines, the regiment opened fire; and there it stood without a support, facing, in a death-struggle, three times its number. The fiery

Creighton received a wound which compelled him to leave the field. The noble Crane was disabled; and the brave Molyneaux, for the moment, took command. Seeing the regiment nearly surrounded, and exposed to an enfilading fire, which was fast thinning the ranks, he ordered it to retreat; but heroic young Clarkey, mistaking it for an order to charge, dashed gallantly forward, at the head of his command. After understanding the order, he had barely time to fall back before the wings of the rebel host closed in.

Slowly and sadly the remaining few of the regiment fell back, keeping their faces to the foe. Only one hundred and sixteen, out of three hundred and seven, returned to the rear unhurt; and many of these were disabled from service by severe exposure to the intense heat of the sun, and lack of water. The regiment retired to a hill, and was not again brought into action during the afternoon. At night, however, it was ordered out on picket. After advancing to Cedar Creek it was challenged, and no one answering, it received a terrible volley from the front and both flanks. It fell back to the cover of a piece of woods, and finally to the rear, about a mile, where it bivouacked.

As night settled upon this field of carnage, Banks' entire corps withdrew to the position it occupied early in the day; but the artillery kept up an intermittent fire until near midnight. General Jackson, from his mountain-top, could see every movement of troops, and was enabled to calculate just how long it would take to re-enforce General Banks. Had he not been so imprudent as to come down from his mountain fastness, and attack the Federal forces after night, his loss would have been comparatively little. But as Banks retired, he moved twelve thousand men on to the battle-field, and kept them there during the night; at the same time advancing one battery through the woods into the open field beyond the battle-ground. From this position it opened on the division of Union troops occupying the advance. As soon as the first flash of his guns was seen, Major Davis, chief of artillery in McDowell's corps, ordered two batteries into position, and opened on the enemy. These batteries, being very close, and getting good range, did fearful havoc among the rebels. It is said that General Hartsuff sighted one of the guns that did the most execution. After the battery had retired, Major Davis' guns shelled the battle-field. The enemy being massed in small space, this fire told fearfully on their ranks. After firing about one hundred shells, and the enemy not responding, Major Davis ordered his guns silenced, little dreaming that he had left more dead rebels on the field than all the random artillery firing of the afternoon.

Many deeds of daring were performed at this battle. Captain Ash, of General Pope's staff, riding up to a battery with an order from the general to stop firing, saw that it was a rebel battery; he, however, had sufficient presence of mind to give the order, and ride off. It was obeyed; the battery ceased to fire, and soon after moved off. Captain Ball, of McDowell's staff, did the same thing, and with a like result.

The following incident is from the pen of a correspondent of an Eastern paper:

"Just after the firing of musketry became interesting, I noticed a private soldier coming off the field, and thinking perhaps he was running away to avoid danger, I rode up to him, when I found he had two fingers of his left hand shot away, and a third dreadfully lacerated. I saw at once that he had at least a hand in the fight. I assisted him to dress his wound as well as my limited knowledge of surgery would permit, he, in the mean time, propping up my pluck by his quaint remarks. Said he: 'I don't care a darn for that third finger, for it warn't of no account, no how; but the 'pinter,' and t'other one, were right good 'uns, and I hate to lose 'em. I shouldn't have come to the rear, if I had been able to load my gun; but I wasn't.' After I had dressed his hand, he looked over in the direction of the firing, and stood a moment. Turning to me, he said: 'Stranger, I wish you would just load up my shooting-iron for me; I want to have a little satisfaction out of them cusses for spilling my fore paw.' I loaded his gun for him, and he started back for the top of the hill at a double-quick, in quest of satisfaction. His name is Lapham, of the Ohio Seventh."

During the action, General Banks was leaning against a tree, when a cannon-ball struck it about eighteen inches above his head, passing entirely through. It has been his singular fortune to meet with many narrow escapes. While riding through Winchester, on his retreat before Jackson, a rebel, from a window above, took deliberate aim at him, but was shot by a private of a Massachusetts regiment before he could fire.

The loss to the regiment in this engagement was very heavy, and shows with what determination it maintained the contest. It went into the engagement with three hundred and seven, rank and file, and came out with a loss in killed and wounded of one hundred and ninety-one,—a loss of more than sixty-two per cent.

The following is the list:

Killed.—Lieutenants, James P. Brisbine, Joseph Ross, Frank Johnson; sergeants, C. P. Bowler, Moses Martin; corporals, J. J. Evans, D. W. Wright; privates, Joseph T. Blackwell, William Adams, Edward Burnet, E. S. Shepherd, Charles G. Hettinger, Charles Masters, Benjamin F. Gill, H. F. Dinger, H. Hight, John J. Hensher, Henry C. Case, M. Eckenroad, N. H. McClurg, C. C. Miller, G. B. Swisher, E. Fox, James Stephenson, Alvin H. Benton, John Manning, Michael Waldof, James Ray, Frank Miller, John Weeland.

Wounded.—Colonel William R. Creighton, Lieut.-Colonel O. J. Crane, Adjutant J. B. Molyneaux, Captain William R. Sterling; lieutenants, Henry B. Eaton, W. D. Braden, S. S. Reed, Marcus Hopkins; sergeants, Z. P. Davie, J. S. Cooper, J. C. Jones, A. S. Allen, Arvin Billings, George W. Barnette, E. M. Lazarus, James R. Carter, E. G. Taylor, G. W. Moore, Charles A. Brooks; corporals, M. D. Holmes, Henry J. Brown, L. Wilson, Joseph Trotier, William E. Smith, Thomas C. Brown, Frank J. Ware, Clark Wilson, C. H. Buxton, Norman L. Norris, F. A. Davis, Albert A. Smith, James Alexander, Benjamin Gridley, W. T. Callors, Robert M. Brisk, A. C. Trimmer, Christopher Nesper, James Grobe; privates, A. M. Clinton, Thomas Sherwood, Edward St. Lawrence, Arthur Laffin, Leonard Walker, Jacob C. Gaycly, F. N. Brund, Abraham Ginter, John G. Parsons, Henry Hatfield, Andrew J. Crippin, Charles E. Preble, John H. Galvin, F. Creque, Philip Kelley, T.

Hammond, E. Lown, William Cammel, John Boyle, James Dixon, Samuel E. Garden, Jacob E. Hine, Benjamin Hasfield, Frank Henrickle, P. E. Hill, William L. Latch, Jacob Marks, Thomas C. Riddle, John Stone, Ernest Zincker, Franklin Gaskill, N. Badger, George Carrathurs, T. P. Dixon, Henry Fairchild, J. M. Rofflige, M. Richmond, Theodore Wilder, Oliver Wise, A. Colwell, William Gardner, John Frank, S. E. Hendrickson, N. R. Holcomb, E. Hobday, W. Lapham, F. Manley, John McAdams, H. H. Rhodes, J. Harnner, Joseph L. Clark, James Kelley, William W. Mecker, Charles Himpson, John Wickham, J. Roberts, J. R. Green, Edward E. Day, Lewis Owens, S. A. Fuller, D. G. Burthroff, J. M. Holcomb, Frank Strong, E. G. Meekins, H. Wallace, M. S. Gibbons, J. Donthit, S. Reed, Arthur Adams, Ezra Brown, Ira M. Barlow, George M. Caldwell, George W. Carter, John Downer, Thomas Ely, Sherman Collinger, Stephen H. Hopkins, Daniel Jones, Perrin D. Loomis, David C. Nunemaker, J. L. Oviatt, G. Russell, N. Twitchell, Ralph Winzenried, John C. Fox, A. Inskeep, James Kincaid, John Lentz, R. D. Murray, John Pollock, E. S. Mathews, A. Shaffer, C. Glendenning, Alfred Jackson, Hiram Deeds, Ira S. Ray, Richard Freeman, Samuel Knap, John Fishcun, James A. Tell, William Kelley, T. D. Williams, Charles Smith, George A. Earl, Maskell Bispham, Frederick Michael, Henry Schmid, John Hammond, William Pfahl, John Pike, George Sahl, George Zipp; George Rogers, musician.

CHAPTER XVI.

The regiment goes into camp at Alexandria, but is soon ordered to the front.—Battle of Antietam.

After the battle of Cedar Mountain, the regiment took part in the memorable retreat of General Pope to the Potomac. During the time, it was not engaged in immediate action; but was exposed, on several occasions, to the shell from the enemy's batteries. After a fatiguing march of sixteen days, it arrived, on the 2d day of September, under the guns of the fortifications around Alexandria. On the following day it was marched to Arlington Heights, to the support of Fort Albany, near which it encamped in a beautiful meadow.

At midnight of the same day an order was received to have the command ready to march at half-past eight on the following morning; but it did not leave, however, until near noon, when, crossing the Potomac to Georgetown, it moved off in the direction of Poolesville, bivouacking at night five miles from Georgetown. On the following morning the command started before day had fairly dawned, and passing through Rockville, bivouacked at night near the place. On the 5th it moved forward, and leaving the small village of Darnstown on the left, formed in line of battle, fronting Poolesville, and awaited the advance of the enemy; but he failing to appear in that direction, but threatening Pennsylvania, by the way of Frederick, the command, on the 9th, broke camp and advanced in five columns towards the latter city. After a brief skirmish, the advance entered the place on the 12th. On the 13th, the regiment crossed the mountains into Pleasant Valley to Middletown. While descending the side of the mountain, the progress of the battle of South Mountain was plainly seen. This engagement was fought by the division of General Cox, of Reno's corps. These troops won great praise for their gallantry and good fighting qualities; and the general, an additional star.

On the 15th, the advance of the Federal army drove the enemy in the direction of Boonesboro', and through the town towards Sharpsburg. Generals Richardson's and Pleasanton's column of cavalry and light artillery proved very annoying to the enemy in this day's retreat.

On the following day, the 16th of September, the rebel army took up its position across Antietam Creek, and there awaited the approach of the Federals.

[1]"This position consisted of a series of sharp points, rising from the bank of the creek, and extending to the rear of Sharpsburg in a succession of ridges; but, when viewed from a point a little in front, has the appearance of table-land, the ravines being undistinguishable. These points or ridges are for the most part surmounted by a heavy copse of timber, which furnished admirable shelter for foot-soldiers; while, with batteries flanking each hill, the position was all that a general could wish for defence.

"Seeing the strength of the position, McClellan sent Hooker's and Sumner's corps around to the left of the enemy's advance position, across Antietam Creek, and, ere the close of day, they had succeeded in driving him fully a mile.

"We had lain down in line of battle, expecting to remain till the morrow. The *tattoo* had sounded, and an impressive silence had settled upon the bivouac, broken only by the tread of the alarm-guard, as he slowly paced his beat, and the occasional passing of an orderly, conveying some order to be executed on the coming day. Not long were we to rest. Our ears were soon assailed with —'*Attention, First brigade!*' and we were soon in line, and moving around to the right, to the support of Hooker and Sumner, where we arrived about one A.M., and bivouacked upon the ground held by the rebels scarce six hours previous. An occasional shot or volley, in an adjoining piece of woods, reminded us of the close proximity of the enemy. Nevertheless, the rest of the night was passed quietly enough by us.

"The morning came, fresh and beautiful; but our *reveille* was not the rattle of the drum, nor the clear notes of the bugle. The day was opened by a fierce volley of musketry, succeeded by another, and yet another, which were soon so continuous as to be blended in one unremittent roll. The struggle had commenced, and the sun that rose shone upon a field already red with blood. Soon the heavy booming of cannon was mingled with the sharp, crackling roll of small-arms, and the din was terrific. Hooker was engaged, and hotly too. We were immediately ordered under arms, and advanced in the direction of the fight. Halting in easy supporting distance, we were given thirty minutes in which to make coffee. At the end of this time the volume of sound perceptibly increased, and was becoming nearer. The rebels were re-enforced, and were slowly driving our men before them. 'Forward,' shouted General Mansfield; and forward we went, in column of division, as cool and regular as on drill. Changing direction to the left, we advanced through a cornfield taken by Hooker the evening previous, and which was now held by the rebels, having driven our boys back. An open field lay before us, commanded by the direct and flank fire of the rebel artillery, and the left flank of their infantry. Notwithstanding the heavy fire we thus suddenly received, the advance was made steadily, and in slow time. Arriving at the front, we deployed into line of battle. The line now being complete, we advanced; *and the work was begun.* No halt was made until the woods were ours; but the enemy was to be dislodged from behind a rail fence. Then we occupied the crest of the hill in the woods, and from this point we directed our fire to the fence, where we could plainly see them level their pieces at us, and fire.

"For an hour and a half we thus remained, and fought: one side with the energy of despair; the other, with an energy imparted with the consciousness of right and justice. The contest was fair and equal, and the right triumphed. At last the line began to waver, and General Green shouted, 'Charge!' With a yell of triumph we started, with levelled bayonets; and, terror-stricken, the rebels fled. Like hounds after the frightened deer, we pursued them fully three-fourths of a mile, killing, wounding, and taking prisoners almost every rod. Their colors fell: a private soldier leaped forward, and tore them from the staff.

"Across the fields we pursued the foe, who again took shelter in a heavy piece of timber, flanked by their artillery. A battery of twelve-pounder howitzers came to our support, and most efficient service it rendered. We formed in two lines in rear of the battery, and lay behind a low ridge, sufficiently high to protect from a direct shot, but which offered no shelter from the fragments of shells bursting near to and over us; these were continually striking amongst us, often grazing a cap or an arm, but doing no particular harm. The howitzers were doing splendidly, when suddenly we heard, 'But eight rounds left!' Twenty more rounds would silence the rebel battery, but we had them not. Soon the rebel fire was more rapid, and a yell in the distance denoted an advance of their infantry. Shall we retreat? No! we will hold our ground, or die! On they come, yelling defiantly: 'tis A. P. Hill's division, second to none but Jackson's. We look anxiously for another battery. It comes! It comes! We are safe! The gallant Eighth Rhode Island Battery comes up in splendid style; our ranks open right and left for them, the exhausted battery of howitzers wheeling out of line. The Parrotts were unlimbered, and shell, five-second fuse, called for, and they opened in glorious style.

"But what means that shout so closely on our right? They have flanked us, and are charging our battery! A half right wheel was made, and we were partially under cover of a narrow ridge. A portion of our front rank, with the colors, advanced, and opened a fire upon their column, but, as it was intended, it only drew them on; shouting fiercely, they dashed forward, expecting to have an easy capture. We waited until they were within six rods, when, with a yell such as freemen know how to give, we rose and poured the contents of our rifles into the mass of graybacks emerging from the woods. They reeled and staggered for a moment, then rallied, and returned our fire for half an hour, then wavered. Perceiving this, Lieutenant-Colonel Tindell, commanding brigade, ordered a charge. As we started, they broke and fled in confusion. Our brigade advanced to the woods, but was soon replaced by a New Jersey regiment, which quickly broke and fled. On came the rebels, yelling and exultingly waving their colors, across a field, and entered a cornfield to the south, to flank our men who were engaging a division. Their triumph was short, for they suddenly found themselves nearly surrounded by General Franklin's troops, who came in from the north and east, over the identical ground we fought over, and precipitated themselves upon the flank of the enemy, six hundred of whom threw down their guns and surrendered, those remaining fleeing in dismay from the field.

"This *coup de grace* closed the heavy fighting upon the right, and we retired from the front, lacerated but cheerful, feeling that our duty was faithfully performed, and knowing that the rebels were defeated."

The next two days were occupied in burying the dead and collecting the wounded.

On the 19th, the regiment left for Harper's Ferry, arriving at Maryland Heights on the 20th. A few days after it forded the Potomac River, and went into permanent camp on Loudon Heights.

The regiment sustained a loss at the battle of Antietam of five killed and thirty-eight wounded. The list is as follows:

Killed.—Sergeant James B. Carter; Corporal Martin Lazrus; privates, John Bacon, Elbridge F. Meachum, George O. Sherick.

Wounded.—Lieutenant Ernest J. Kreiger; sergeants, George A. McKay, Jerry G. Clafflin, Isaac Jones, James Hansell; corporals, Edward Goodsell, Henry H. Bailey, Hiram J. Bell, John F. Ely, Austin Bull, James Bryant, J. Kurly; privates, George A. Wood, Joseph Kubler, Laurine Lamphier, Pliney E. Hill, George Steinberger, E. C. Miller, Daniel Weatherlow, David Everett, Alfred W. Mosley, Averett C. Reed, Alson Coe, Alfred E. May, Thomas Woolf, Henry Wilcox, George Houck, William Cromwell, Caleb Bryant, George Wandal, Nick Bauer, Charles Briedenbach, Charles Graiter.

CHAPTER XVII.

The march to Dumfries.—Skirmish with Hampton's cavalry, in which they are badly defeated by a much inferior force.

While at Loudon Heights, the monotony of life in camp was relieved by drill, guard, and picket duty, with an occasional reconnoissance. On the latter occasions some little skirmishing would usually occur. An occasional dash was made by the rebels upon the Union picket-line.

Soon after the occupation of this post the grand army crossed the Potomac and Shenandoah into the Loudon Valley, on its way to Fredericksburg. We copy a description of the march of a regiment in Porter's corps.[2]

"I have been thinking of the difference between soldiering that we read about—fancy soldiering, glory and honor soldiering—and real soldiering of the rough and tumble kind. How well it sounds to read: 'A regiment of brave men marched proudly through the streets of Harper's Ferry, to strains of sweet music. Gallantly the veterans of a dozen battles streamed along, their banners gayly floating in the breeze; they go to join the Army of the Potomac.' What is it when divested of its trimmings? 'About three hundred and fifty of what once was a regiment one thousand strong, went through Harper's Ferry to-day. In vain the tum, tum, tum of the drum, at the head of the column, urged the men to keep time. Wearied, worn out by continued tramping, loaded down with their knapsacks, three days' rations in their haversacks, and the prospect of a long march before them, slowly they dragged themselves along; their torn and tattered flag, as well as soiled clothes, giving evidence of hard service.' Again let us quote: 'At evening they halted, and bivouacked for the night; refreshed and ready at early dawn to continue the line of march.' Sift that a little—that bivouac. Almost worn out with incessant and continued tramping through mud, and muck, and mire, great clumps of which would stick and cleave on to the shoe at every step, the night fast closing in, the column halted; slowly the lingering mass closed up, stacked arms, and broke ranks. Some, too tired to make a fire and cook food, threw themselves on the cold, damp ground, and, with their blankets wrapped around them, shivered to sleep; others, having eaten scarcely any thing all day, threw off their cumbrous loads, and started, in the now dark night, in search of wood and water. An old fire-scorched tin cup answers for a coffee-pot as well as tea-kettle. Into it the water, muddy with the feet of perhaps a thousand water-hunting tired ones, is put; and while the coffee is boiling, a piece of fat pork is drawn from the haversack, and a slice cut off; a long stick, pointed, on which the slice is secured, and frizzling, sizzling, half burned, half cooked, ready when the coffee is. The pork, coffee, and hard bread form, for the hundredth time, the meal of the hungry soldier. Perhaps on the roadside, right in the mud, glad in truth to lie anywhere, one after another drops his wearied form. The heavy rain comes down in torrents, wetting him through and through, but tired nature heeds it not—must have rest.

"Early dawn comes. Again the pork, coffee, and hard bread; and the stiffened, sore, leg-weary patriot buckles on his saturated knapsack, and, like a foundered horse, limps achingly along till he gets heated up, with the same prospect before him of twenty miles tramp—clamp—tramp."

On the 10th day of December the regiment left Bolivar Heights, crossed the Shenandoah on a pontoon, and winding round the bluff of Loudon, passed up the Loudon Valley.

While passing through Hillsboro', the command was given, by Lieutenant Shepherd to his men, to "Close up!—get into your places!" General Geary, on foot and unobserved, had marched along just in rear of the company. Hearing the command, he remarked: "Well, here is a vacant place, I guess I'll fill it up;" and stepped into the place. He marched, in this manner, some distance, talking freely with those nearest him, at the same time obeying orders promptly.

The regiment encamped about a mile beyond Hillsboro'.

Bright and early on the following morning the command moved on. Leaving the battle-field where the brave Kearney fell, and Fairfax on the left, on the 15th it arrived in sight of the Lower Potomac, and encamped after crossing Naabsco Creek.

Having passed Dumfries on the 17th, an order came that the Fifth, Seventh, and Sixty-sixth regiments, under command of Colonel Candy, should march back and hold that post. On the following day, crossing Powell's Creek, two hours' march brought the brigade in the outskirts of Dumfries, where it went into camp.

Nothing transpired worthy of mention until the 27th of December, when the heavy booming of cannon was heard in the vicinity of the picket-line. It was evident that the enemy were making a descent on the pickets. For several days this attack had been expected, therefore in a few minutes the command was ready and in line of battle. The pickets gradually gave way, under the command of the indomitable Creighton, fighting their way back to the line of battle, in which they took position. The rebels came gallantly forward, in anticipation of an easy victory. When within short-range of our guns, they were met by such a terrible fire of musketry from our partially concealed line, as to check their advance. They, however, rallied, and returned the fire; but in a moment staggered, and finally withdrew in confusion from the field. Again forming their broken columns, they hurled themselves against our line. They were again met by a determined front, and, with a like result, were sent, broken and mangled, back upon their reserves. A third time reforming their wasted ranks, they came down with great impetuosity, and hurled their solid columns against the weak lines of the Federals. They were again met with a sheet of flame, which sent up its column of blue smoke along the entire front. For a moment it was impossible to tell the effect produced on the rebels; but the smoke clearing away before a light breeze, it was discovered that their advance had been arrested. One more united effort, and the rebel line was again sent back crushed and bleeding. They again organized for a last desperate charge, and most gallantly did they sweep down upon our line. Up the hill and over the brush and logs, which lay in their way, with wild impetuosity, which threatened to crush every thing before them. Aware of the avalanche that was sweeping down upon them, the Union boys hugged the ground, awaiting, with breathless anxiety, the command to fire. At last the stentorian voice of the sturdy Crane was heard to shout the order, when a band of patriots, their eyes kindled to a blaze with the ardor of their daring, with strong muscles and steady nerves, rose, and with a shout that made the gray hills of old Dumfries echo, poured a volley of death into the rebel host. Disdaining to again take refuge under cover, the line stood manfully up, and met the continued onsets of the foe. The brave Creighton stood on a hill exposed to the fire—how could men falter while the noble form of their leader was thus bared to the bullets of the enemy? They did not falter; but the line stood like a wall. The rebels were soon seen to waver, and as the night "cast its mantle over the combatants," they tardily and solemnly withdrew, bearing with them the lacerated, bleeding victims to their endurance.

At night the line was drawn in, and after making every effort for the security of the command, the boys lay down upon their arms, harassed by an oppressive uncertainty which always haunts the soldier in the bivouac upon the battle-field.

During that long night the lonely picket-guard peered out into the darkness, intent upon catching the first footfall of the cautious foe. Slowly and with careful tread he paced his weary beat, fearful that he might be pounced upon by the wily enemy ere he could give the alarm to his slumbering companions. Through rain, and sleet, and darkness—oppressed with the solemn stillness that at night hangs over the earth—with a sense of loneliness weighing upon his feelings—he stood like a spectre in the gloom, the guardian of the thousands slumbering in the camp. While others dream of home, and friends, and firesides, afar off on the hills of New England, or the starlit prairies of the West, the wakeful picket keeps his vigil. May God protect him in his watch!

As day again dispelled the shadows that darkened the hills and the valleys, the columns of the brave Sigel were seen winding their way through the village. A shout of welcome greeted these heroes. The dreadful suspense that had weighed upon the hearts of the combatants of the day before, during that long night of watching, now gave place to cheerfulness; and confidence was again restored. But the cautions Hampton had fled; and nothing met the eye save the frowning hills.

The following is the list of killed and wounded in this affair:

Killed.—Corporal Austin Ball.

Wounded.—Corporal E. M. Corrdett; privates, Sylvester Carter, Philip Grigsby, Thomas Roff, Wm. P. Root, Wm. H. Kibbee, W. M. Perry, Stephen Willock.

Prisoners.—John Gordon, Andrew Atleff, Richard M. Vreeland, Douglass F. Pomeroy, Henry T. Benton, Lewis T. Butts, Henry Alderman, Charles Bradly, James Snider, John Beiler, W. M. Perry.

CHAPTER XVIII.

The regiment ordered to the front.—Battle of Chancellorsville.

Near the middle of April, 1863, the regiment marched down to Aquia Landing, where it remained in camp for two weeks.

General Hooker was now in command of the grand Army of the Potomac, having relieved Burnside after that general's unsuccessful attack on Fredericksburg. Hooker resolved to make an attempt to drive the rebel army from the vicinity of the Rappahannock. Burnside's failure had demonstrated the impracticability of crossing the river at Fredericksburg; for no army was safe for a moment with a strong army behind three lines of well-constructed earthworks in its front, and a wide and deep river in its rear. He therefore chose a flank movement by the way of Banks and United States fords, thus striking the left flank of the enemy near Chancellorsville Court-house, and avoiding their strong fortifications in the rear of Fredericksburg.

The Seventh Regiment arrived in the vicinity of Chancellorsville on the afternoon of the 30th of April, and encamped for the night a little southeast of the latter place, and near the Fredericksburg plankroad.

Early on Friday morning it was ordered forward, and took position in the second line of battle, in an open wood-lot, facing south. Late in the afternoon it was ordered back; and it finally took position directly south of the famous brick house, called the Chancellorsville Place, where headquarters were established and maintained during most of the action.

Just before dark the rebels came up in great numbers, in an attack on Knapp's Battery, which was stationed on the left. The Seventh was ordered to its support, but the attack was repelled before the regiment became warmly engaged. It remained in support of this battery during the night and in the forenoon of the following day. About noon of the 2d of May, the regiment was ordered forward to support a line of skirmishers; but this line, refusing to advance, was passed by the regiment, when it took the advance, and most handsomely drove the enemy back for some distance, holding the ground for several hours, when it was ordered to retire. It did so without confusion, taking a new position in rear of a piece of woods, where it remained until ordered into the intrenchments.

During this advance, the right wing was hotly engaged, and lost heavily; the left wing suffering slightly. It remained during the night in its old position near the brick house, in the second line of battle.

On the 3d, the regiment advanced to what is known as "the old rifle-pit," which it occupied while the other troops were falling back across a cleared field south of the Fredericksburg plankroad. Here it was exposed to a galling fire from the advancing rebel column; but it stood firm. When the balance of the troops of the brigade were in proper position, it formed under the protection of a battery, and slowly moved off the field, exposed to a terrible fire of both musketry and artillery, taking up its position in rear of the brigade. The brigade, however, was soon driven back, and passed to the rear of the regiment, exposing it to a severe fire. Soon the order came for a general advance, when the brigade, with a loud shout, dashed at the foe, led by the Seventh. The rebels were pushed back for a considerable distance; but no support coming up, the brigade was compelled to fall back to the south of the brick house, where it halted, and laid down in the road; but about eleven o'clock at night the shelling became so continuous and heavy that it was forced still further back, and finally resulting in its withdrawal to the vicinity of United States Ford. That night the regiment occupied a rifle-pit about half a mile from the river. At four o'clock in the afternoon of the 5th, it was relieved by the Fifth Ohio; and taking a circuitous route, arrived in a ravine on the left of the column, and near the river, and was soon after employed in the intrenchments.

Early in the morning of the 6th, the regiment crossed the river on a pontoon at United States Ford, and in the afternoon of the 7th arrived at its old camp at Aquia Landing.

In this battle the regiment was actively engaged but a small portion of the time. The loss was not severe, when taking into account the magnitude of the engagement, and its duration.

Why the army recrossed the river has not been fully explained. The immediate battle was not a defeat; at least it has not been considered as such. However, the two columns of Sedgwick and Hooker failed to unite, which fact may have had an influence in determining the retreat. The attacks of the enemy had been repulsed at all points, while Sedgwick had carried a portion of their fortifications in rear of Fredericksburg. The retreat alone turned a prospective victory into a humiliating defeat. The grand army failed to accomplish the purpose of its advance, and was compelled to hasten its march across the river in retreat, over which it had, but a week before, advanced in triumph. It can be said by way of apology only, that while at Chancellorsville the army maintained its reputation for bravery and endurance, the enemy manifestly looked upon it as a fruitless victory to him.

The following is a list of the killed and wounded:

Killed.—Orderly-Sergeant Henry Whiting; Color-Sergeant John D. Creigh; Corporal A. C. Trimmer; privates, Charles H. Cheeney, E. N. Larom, Henry A. Pratt, John Randle, Almon Lower, John Lee, Stafford Penney, Thomas Carle, A. C. Steadman, Victor Perrley, Henry Ackman.

Wounded.—Orderly-Sergeant Elmon Hingston; sergeants, H. H. Bailey, John S. Davis, James Lapham, H. L. Allen; corporals, A. A. Austin, John Gardiner, S. M. Cole, J. S. Kellogg; privates, W. Furniss, H. Owen, F. Eldridge, W. Van Wye, E. C. Palmer, D. L. Hunt, E. V. Nash, Henry H. Pierce, O. Jackman, C. A. Wood, H. S. Smalley, Charles P. Smith, S. P. Sherley, F. Rockefellow, Frank Randal, Joseph Kubler, Michael St. Auge, David Boil, James Dixon, Oliver Wise, James Farron, G. Breakman, F. Mauley, John Shelby, Andrew Copeland, S. G. Cone, W. W. Hunt, E. Kennedy, H. G. Benton, A. S. Raymond, C. A. Parks, Isaac Stratton, H. Thwing, James Baxter, J. W. Benson, S. Hughes, P. Smith, S. A. Fuller, F. Hank, John Clonde, E. O. Whiting, G. W. Bonn, S. H. Barnum, J. C. Brooks, W. H. Fox, I. H. Gregg, W. Hunter, H. Jones, S. Moneysmith, S. S. Pelton, B. Wilson, D. W. Waters, W. H. Bannister, H. Lewis, W. J. Evans, C. L. Cowden, H. Hoffman, S. Renz, M. Saiser, E. A. Spurn, L. Knoble.

CHAPTER XIX.

Accompanies the grand army into Pennsylvania.—Battle of Gettysburg.

After the battle of Chancellorsville, the regiment remained for some time in its camp at Aquia Landing. The Army of the Potomac, as well as that of Lee, was quietly reorganizing, preparatory to another struggle. Soon Lee began to threaten the outer line of Hooker, by making demonstrations on the various fords of the Rappahannock. At one time threatening to move boldly across, and at another menacing the flank, as if to attack one wing of the army. These various movements gave rise to sharp skirmishes, nothing more. At last it was evident that Lee meant an invasion of the North. The Army of the Potomac was therefore set in motion.

The Seventh left its camp early in June, and proceeded to Martinsburg by the way of Fairfax. Lee continuing his flank movement, the grand army was compelled to fall back across the Potomac; the Seventh crossing at Edward's Ferry. The rebel army now crossed the river by the way of Williamsport, and moved forward towards Pennsylvania. The Army of the Potomac moved in the same direction, passing through Frederick City, Maryland, and taking up its position in rear of Gettysburg, Pennsylvania. The line of battle was formed a little distance from and facing the town. On the first day of July the rebel army advanced and occupied the town, but the day was exhausted in manœuvring, attended with slight skirmishing between the advance of the two armies.

Hooker had been relieved, and General Meade ordered to assume command.

After the Seventh arrived on the field it took its position on the left side of the Gettysburg and Littletown pike.

Early on the morning of the 2d it took a position on a hill on the right of this road, at the same time sending Company H to the front, under command of Captain McClelland. This company remained at the front during the entire day. For the first time in its history, the regiment occupied a position under cover, a stone wall being in its front. Up to this time it had not been exposed to the fire of infantry; but during the afternoon it suffered slight loss from a brisk artillery fire. At eleven o'clock at night it advanced down the pike, and took a position in a hollow, running at right angles with the road. It was now exposed to a musketry fire, resulting in the wounding of one man. It soon fell back to a stone wall, parallel with a road leading to the pike; and shortly after it advanced to this road, from which twenty men were sent forward as skirmishers, under command of Sergeant Stratton. This gallant soldier was mortally wounded while bravely leading his command against the foe.

On the morning of the 3d the regiment moved forward, after having called in the skirmishers, to the relief of the Sixtieth New York Volunteers, occupying a line of intrenchments. In the evening it was relieved, and withdrew to the breastworks in the rear; but was soon after ordered forward to the relief of another regiment, where it remained until late in the evening. During the entire day it was exposed to a heavy fire of musketry, from which it suffered considerable loss, considering the position it occupied. When relieved, it withdrew to the position held by it in the morning.

At one o'clock on the morning of the 4th of July, it again moved forward to the intrenchments, where it remained till the brigade moved off in the direction of Littletown.

The following incidents occurred July the 3d: While occupying the intrenchments, a white flag was seen flying from the front of the enemy's lines. The firing being suspended, seventy-eight rebels came forward and surrendered, including six officers. Lieutenant Leigh, of Ewell's staff, came forward and endeavored to stop the surrender; but was fired upon by the regiment, and instantly killed.

Corporal John Pollock leaped over the breastworks and captured the flag of the Fourteenth Virginia rebel regiment.

Private James J. Melton was wounded, and afterwards taken to a hospital, where he remained for some time; since which his friends have heard nothing from him. The wound being in the head, he is supposed to have become deranged and wandered away, unable to give any account of himself. No means have been left untried to obtain information of his whereabouts, but without avail.

The regiment having fought under partial cover, the loss was slight: one killed and seventeen wounded.

CHAPTER XX.

After reaching the Rapidan it goes to Governor's Island.—After its return it accompanies Hooker's corps to the Western department.

After the battle of Gettysburg, the regiment was with the grand army in pursuit of the broken columns of General Lee. Passing through Frederick City, it arrived at Harper's Ferry and went into camp. Here it remained for two days, when it moved across the Potomac, and again passing up the beautiful Loudon Valley, crossed the Blue Ridge to Fairfax and Manassas Junction, over the old battle-field of Bull Run. Again taking up the line of march, it crossed the Rappahannock below Culpepper Court-house, and encamped on the banks of the Rapidan.

About this time a riot broke out in New York city, which required the presence of the military, as an assistance to the civil authorities. The Government was therefore called upon to furnish troops. Several regiments were at once dispatched to the scene of strife. Among these was the Seventh. It left the vicinity of the Rapidan about one week after its arrival there. It marched to Alexandria, and there taking the United States ship Baltic, passed down the Potomac through Chesapeake Bay to the ocean, arriving on Governor's Island in the latter part of August. It remained until the first of September, when again embarking, it sailed to Alexandria, from whence it marched to the Rapidan, near its old camp.

General Rosecrans had now been removed from the command of the Army of the Cumberland, and General Grant assumed control. The army occupied the vicinity of Chattanooga, Tennessee; while the rebel army under General Bragg occupied Mission Ridge, immediately in front of and overlooking the city. The task of driving Bragg from this position was assigned to General Grant.

Before entering upon this campaign, however, it was necessary to re-enforce the Army of the Cumberland; for it had not entirely recovered from the disastrous battle of Chickamauga. For this purpose it was necessary to draw on the Army of the Potomac, now lying idle on the banks of the Rapidan. At this time this army had, *positively* speaking, accomplished nothing. It had barely saved Washington from the enemy. To be sure, it had seen many hard-fought battles, and on all occasions sustained its reputation for courage and endurance. But the results following these battles were entirely negative; and after more than two years of marches, counter-marches, sieges, and battles, when graves had been dug from the Potomac to the James, and filled with the best blood of the land, and the country left in mourning for her fallen braves, but little territory had been gained, and the possession of this little being constantly disputed by a well-organized and gallant army. A sort of fatality had thus settled down upon the Army of the Potomac. Some of the best generals had been summoned to its command, but to no purpose. The hand of fate rested upon it heavily. When about to seize upon victory, some stream would rise in its rear, or some unseen accident happen to its communications or line of supplies, compelling it to let go its hold on victory, and in its stead to accept defeat. No wonder, then, that the authorities saw fit to send a part of this not very promising army to a department where victory sometimes rested upon the Federal arms. Hooker's corps was therefore ordered to report to Grant.

The Seventh being a part of this command, left its camp on the Rapidan in the latter part of September, and moving up to Washington, passed over to the Baltimore and Ohio Railroad, when it left for Nashville, Tennessee, by the way of Columbus, Indianapolis, and Louisville. It soon after left for Wartrays, by the way of Murfreesboro'. It was now ordered to construct winter-quarters, but having them nearly completed, it was ordered to Bridgeport, Alabama, where it arrived in due time.

This entire trip from the East was accomplished without any delay, and nothing occurring to lessen the good opinion the people entertained for this veteran corps.

CHAPTER XXI.

The Seventh joins Grant's army.—The battles of Lookout Mountain, Mission Ridge, and Ringgold.

After remaining for some time at Bridgeport, the regiment was ordered to the vicinity of Lookout Mountain. It marched to the little village of Wahatcha, at the base of this mountain, and went into camp. It remained, however, but a short time, and then returned to Bridgeport, where it went into permanent camp.

Late in the fall, General Grant had perfected his arrangements to attack the rebel stronghold on Lookout Mountain; and, as a preparatory measure, his vast army was concentrated in the vicinity of Chattanooga. An immense quantity of stores had been gathered, while garrisons were placed at points to be held for the purpose of keeping up communication with the army after its advance. Early in November, the Seventh left its quarters in Alabama, and joined the grand army.

On the 24th of November, the army was set in motion. The Seventh passed up the northern slope of the mountain, and crossing Lookout Creek, formed in line of battle. It now steadily advanced, arriving at the rebel camp to find it in the hands of our men. But desultory firing was kept up by the rebel sharpshooters concealed in the timber and behind rocks on the summit of the mountain. The regiment was now ordered on picket. Passing around to the east side of the mountain, it was fired upon by the enemy; but owing to their being entirely hidden from view by the dense fog that had settled over the combatants, it did not return the fire, but secured a safe harbor behind rocks and trees. This fire was kept up for nearly two hours, with a loss to the regiment of only four men wounded. Before night the regiment was relieved from duty and marched to the rear, bivouacking in a peach orchard.

About ten A.M. of the 25th, it moved down the opposite side of the mountain, and passing through a small valley, soon reached Mission Ridge. Without halting, the command moved steadily up this mountain, and on arriving on its summit, found that the rebels had fled. Passing into another valley, it bivouacked for the night. On the 26th, the command moved to the vicinity of Pigeon Mountain, where it remained till the following day. Early on the morning of the 27th, it moved on to Ringgold, Georgia, where it found the enemy securely posted on Taylor's Ridge. On arriving in this town, the brigade was ordered to scale the mountain. It was formed on the railroad, in two lines of battle; the second line being ordered to preserve a distance of one hundred yards. Two Pennsylvania regiments formed the first line, and the Sixty-sixth and Seventh Ohio the second line; the Seventh being on the left. The enemy soon discovered the intention of our troops, and made his dispositions to meet the attack by extending his right. As soon as the advance began, the enemy opened fire. Arriving at the foot of the hill, the first line halted to return the fire, and the second line passed through. The Seventh now moved into a ravine, where it was exposed to a terrible fire from the front and both flanks, but it pressed on without firing a shot. Arriving almost on the crest of the hill, the fire became too effective for even these gallant veterans to withstand, and the line gave way, fighting as it went. In this manner, the surviving few reached the foot of the hill.

This engagement was short, but terrible in its results to the regiment. It may be said that with this struggle its star of glory began to fade—its pride and spirit were broken. But one officer escaped uninjured, while many were killed. The number of men in the action was two hundred and six, of whom fourteen was killed and forty-nine wounded.

For what purpose this handful of men were ordered to storm the enemy's position on the hill has never been explained. There was no artillery used to cover the assault, without which it was impossible to carry the position with such a force, and hazardous to attempt it with any. Within a short distance there was a large amount of artillery, which could have been placed in position, after which Taylor's Ridge would have been untenable by the enemy. On seeing such dispositions being made, he would probably have anticipated the movement, and fled without firing a gun. But thus far Hooker and his almost invincible corps had carried every thing before them. This success seemed to bring with it a contempt for the rebel soldiers, which finally resulted in the great disaster at Taylor's Ridge. A good general will resist the influences growing out of success, and not be led by these to undertake impossibilities, and by such rashness endanger that which he has already gained. It requires greater self-control to resist the temptations following victory, than to overcome the demoralizing influences of defeat. Victory must never elate a general, while defeat must never depress him.

After this battle, an unsuccessful attempt was made to get the regiment ordered home. But the response of Halleck, to a similar application, made after the battle of Cedar Mountain, was reiterated. "No!" said the old warrior; "not so long as there is a lame drummer-boy left; not if you will send us a whole new regiment in place of this handful. We know these men—they are just such as we want." This compliment, from an officer who was in command of all of the armies of the United States, was worth many a hard march, as well as battle.

The following is a list of the killed and wounded in the three battles of Lookout Mountain, Mission Ridge, and Taylor's Ridge:

Killed.—Colonel W. R. Creighton; Lieutenant-Colonel O. J. Crane; Adjutant Moris Baxter; second-lieutenants, Isaac C. Jones and Joseph Cryne; sergeants, J. C. Corlet, William Van Wye; corporals, Alfred Austin, W. H. Bennett; privates, C. F. King, C. E. Wall, D. P. Wood, J. L. Fish, Thomas Sweet, Oliver Grinels, Lawrence Remmel, H. Hanson, J. H. Merrill, William Pfuel.

Wounded.—Captains, W. D. Braden, Samuel McClelland; first-lieutenants, George A. McKay, George D. Lockwood; second-lieutenants, D. H. Brown, E. H. Bohm, H. N. Spencer, Christian Nesper; sergeants, M. M. Cutler, John Gardner, L. Wilson, Isaac Stratton, Elmore Hemkston; corporals, James W. Raymond, E. V. Nash, John Baptee, C. Glendenning, Hiram Deeds, Thomas Dowse, George Spencer, William Senfert, J. E. Hine, W. H. Petton, J. H. Cleverton, H. C. Hunt, M. H. Sheldon, John Phillips, W. O. Barnes, M. Fitzgerald, J. Tuttle, George Eikler, W. J. Lowrie, H. O. Pixley, W. H. Johnson, John Bergin, W. Wise, H. B. Pownell, J. N. Hall, V. Reynolds, R. White, H. Wright, R. D. Gates, Otis Martin, Joseph Kincaid, W. O. Johnson, J. Decker, J. Hall, C. Cowden, D. F. Dow, George Mandall, H. Fezer, George Raynette, L. Habbig, John Schwinck, Joseph Rowe, C. Deitz.

The following were wounded at Lookout Mountain:

John H. Galvin, M. C. Stone, M. W. Bartlett, James A. Garrison, Louis Owen, A. Gordon.

CHAPTER XXII.

The advance towards Atlanta.—Skirmishing.—Homeward march.—Its reception.—Muster out.

The series of successes in the vicinity of Chattanooga made Grant a lieutenant-general, and gave Sherman the command of the armies in Tennessee. Preparations were now made to press back the forces marshalled in rebellion at all points. Early in the spring the ball was opened in the East by Lieutenant-General Grant in person, while in the West the indomitable Sherman set his invincible army in motion towards the very heart of the so-called Confederacy. The advance was sounded, and the Union hosts pressed onward.

By sunset on the 17th of May the Seventh Regiment reached Calhoun, and on the 19th the vicinity of Cassville, where it hastily threw up some breastworks; but after two hours was ordered forward in line of battle. On the 23d it passed through the latter village, across the railroad, and at four P.M., arrived on the banks of the Etawa River; and after fording the stream, bivouacked for the night. On the 25th it took the advance of the entire column, and deployed seven companies as skirmishers. The march of these companies was very toilsome, and their progress correspondingly slow. Near Pumpkin Vine Creek the advance was fired upon by the enemy's pickets, and a sharp skirmish ensued. During this time the enemy attempted to destroy the bridge over the creek, but were driven back by the regiment; when it immediately crossed, and took possession of a commanding hill.

Generals Hooker and Geary, with staff and body-guard, had moved forward with the skirmish-line, and sometimes in advance even of this. On one of the latter occasions the body-guard was fired upon, and the three reserve companies of the Seventh were ordered to their relief.

The advance of the enemy was now held in check until the other regiments of the brigade came up, when he was dispersed.

In this skirmish, one man was killed and eight wounded. At this point the command threw up some breastworks, where it remained until six P.M., when it advanced in line of battle. In this movement the regiment became hotly engaged, losing three killed and fifteen wounded. One of the enemy's shell exploding in the ranks, occasioned the loss of eight men. On the 28th and the previous night, considerable skirmishing was kept up in front of the line of intrenchments, as well as some sharp artillery firing; which, however, did very little damage. These pieces were soon silenced by a New York battery. All day and night of the 30th the regiment was engaged in sharp skirmishing; but one man, however, was injured, and he severely. On the 2d of June it moved forward to Allatoona, Georgia, where it built breastworks, and went into camp.

Here it remained for some time, when its term of service having expired, it hastened its steps homeward; thus severing the connecting link between it and the army. The members of this veteran regiment now felt that they were no longer soldiers: that, although they retained the organization and uniform of a regiment, they were private citizens hastening to enjoy home and friends, from which they had been so long separated. They marched with joyous hearts, and yet there was sadness present with this happiness. Many a comrade was left behind, never to return. Fresh graves marked its line of march from Chattanooga to Georgia. Friends and kindred were sleeping beneath these green mounds, and they could not pass them by, in this homeward march, without a tear of regret.

Following the line of the railroad, the regiment finally halted and awaited transportation. When this was furnished, it went to Nashville by railroad, at which place it embarked on steamers and started down the Cumberland River. Arriving in the vicinity of Harpeth Shoals, it was fired on by guerrillas, and two men wounded. Both officers and men were desirous of landing and punishing this band of outlaws for their insolence, but could not prevail on the captain of the boat to permit it.

Arriving in the Ohio River, Sergeant Trembly fell from the boat and was drowned. This was a sad occurrence. He had served faithfully during the service of the regiment; and now, on the eve of being mustered out, he lost his life by accident. The boat was stopped, and efforts made to rescue him, but without success.

When the regiment reached Cincinnati, the Fifth Ohio had already arrived. The city being about to give an ovation to this gallant regiment, the Seventh was invited to take part in it, by partaking of the hospitality of the city. This demonstration, in honor of the two regiments, was eminently fitting, for they were united by the ties of long fellowship. From the very first they had been brigaded together. The history of the one was the history of the other. They had marched, bivouacked, and fought side by side. Each prized the honor and renown of the other not less than its own. The city of Cincinnati, in thus extending its hospitality to the Seventh Regiment, did much credit to itself. The friends of the regiment will remember this magnanimous conduct, while the members of the regiment will keep green the memory of the gallant Fifth.

The following is from the Cleveland Herald, of the 11th of June:

"On Saturday afternoon, soon after the evening papers had been issued, a dispatch was received, announcing that the Seventh Ohio had but just left Cincinnati, and would not arrive in Cleveland until about seven o'clock Sunday morning. Bulletins to this effect were at once printed, and distributed through the city; but a large crowd of persons, not aware of this fact, came down to watch the arrival of the evening train, on which the Seventh was supposed to be coming.

"On Sunday morning the population of the city were early astir, and by seven o'clock a large and continually increasing crowd had assembled in and around the depot. The police, in full uniform, marched down to the depot, and were followed by the old members of the Seventh, bearing the second regimental flag, the first having been deposited in the State-house at Columbus.

"At seven o'clock the ringing of the fire-bells announced the approach of the time for the arrival of the train; and about half-past seven o'clock a salute from the guns, manned by the Brooklyn Artillery, and run down to the bluff at the foot of Water-street, announced the arrival of the train.

"As it moved into the depot it was received with cheers by the assembled crowd; and the war-worn veterans were soon out of the cars, and surrounded by anxious and joyful friends. Shouts of welcome, hearty hand-shaking, embraces and kisses, were showered upon the sun-browned soldiers. Many of the scenes were very affecting. In one place a young wife, whose husband had left for the field just after their marriage, hung with clinging embrace on her returned brave, and her moist eyes sought his with unutterable affection, her hands trembling with excess of joy. In another, an old man, with both hands grasped in those of his son, mingled smiles of joy over his returned boy, with tears of sorrow for the one who had laid down his life for his country. Mothers clung to sons, sisters to brothers, wives to husbands, and some little children climbed up for a father's embrace.

"The number all told, men and officers, of those who returned, was two hundred and forty-five. These were the remnants of nearly eleven hundred men, who left Camp Dennison three years ago, on the reorganization of the regiment. The whole number of the regiment is five hundred and one, of whom the remainder were recruited at various times, and their term of service not expired. Sixty of these were left in Sherman's army; the rest are scattered in every direction, from the James River to Atlanta. The greater part of those whose term of service has not expired are to be consolidated with the same class in the Fifth

Ohio, which fought by its side in many a bloody fray, and which is to retain its number. The slightly wounded were brought up with the regiment, the more seriously wounded being left in different hospitals.

"The following is the present organization of the Seventh:

"Lieutenant-colonel, Sam. McClelland; surgeon, Dr. Bellows; assistant surgeon, Dr. Ferguson; Captain Wilcox, Company E; Captain Kreiger, Company K; Captain Clark, Company B; Captain Howe, Company A; Captain Braden, Company G; Captain Davis, Company C, taken prisoner in last fight; Captain Nesper, Company H; Captain McKay, Company F; Captain Lockwood, Company D; Lieutenant Bohm, commanding Company I; quartermaster, S. D. Loomis.

"The regiment left Chattanooga with the Fifth Ohio; but parted company on the way, the Fifth having left their arms behind them, and were therefore compelled to come by railroad, no unarmed troops being allowed to come by the river. The Seventh came up the Cumberland and Ohio rivers by steamboats, and were fired on by guerrillas on the way. One man was lost, Sergeant Trembly, of Company C, about thirty miles below Cincinnati. He was on the guards of the steamer cleaning his gun, when he fell overboard. The boat was stopped, and efforts made to save him; but he was carried away by the current and drowned.

"On reaching Cincinnati, they were ordered to Columbus to be mustered out; but when the train got to Columbus, they were ordered to go on to this city to be paid, and mustered out.

"After leaving the cars, and the greetings of friends were ended, the men were marched to one part of the depot, and given a chance to wash themselves. They were then conducted to tables set along the north wing of the depot, where a hot breakfast had been provided by Wheeler and Russel, on the order of the military committee. Rev. Mr. Goodrich invoked the blessing.

"A number of ladies were on hand, who supplied the soldiers bountifully with strawberries, after the more substantial part of the feast was concluded.

"As soon as the men had been properly fed and refreshed, they fell into line, and proceeded through Water and Superior streets to the front of the government buildings, where the formal reception was to take place. The procession was headed by the police, followed by a brass band, and by the military committee, members of the council, and city officers. The old members of the Seventh, with the second flag of the regiment, tattered and torn, immediately preceded the bronzed veterans, who, fully armed, and bearing their last flag, rent with a hailstorm of hostile bullets, marched with proud steps through the streets they had left three years and three months since. Carriages followed with the sick and wounded who were unable to march. The procession was accompanied with a throng of people, and crowds lined the streets, whilst flags fluttered in all directions.

"On reaching the front of the government building, the regiment was drawn up in double line, and Prosecuting-Attorney Grannis, in the absence of Mayor Senter, addressed the regiment, in behalf of the corporation and citizens, as follows:

"Soldiers of the Seventh Ohio—The people of the city of Cleveland welcome you home. More than three years ago, you went forth with full ranks—more than a thousand strong. To-day a little remnant returns to receive the greetings of friends, and to mingle again with society, as was your wont in times gone by. But this is not all. You, and those who went with you, whether present here to-day or absent, whether among the living or the dead, shall be held forever in grateful remembrance.

"We witnessed your departure with pride, not unmingled with sorrow. We did not regret that the men of the glorious Seventh had gone out to fight against a brutal and insolent foe, or fear that any member of it would ever fail to do his whole duty in the perilous ridges of the battle; but we did know that your departure was attended with many sacrifices;—that you would be exposed to cold, fatigue, and hunger; would suffer from disease, from honorable wounds, and in loathsome prisons; and that many a noble form would bite the dust. We knew that these things must needs be, that the nation might live. The half was not told us. It did not enter into our hearts to believe what you would suffer and what you would accomplish. Upon almost every battle-field, from Cross Lanes to Dalton, the glorious banner of the Seventh has been in the van of the battle. We have watched your course with painful interest. After every battle, came the intelligence that your regiment had fought bravely, and had come out with thinned ranks.

"You have the grand consolation of knowing that the victories of Gettysburg, of Lookout Mountain, of Ringgold, and of Resaca, were not won without your aid. To have been in any one of those desperate conflicts, is glory enough for any man. The record you have made will seem almost like a tale of fiction. We have often had tidings of you, but such as would not cause our cheeks to tingle with shame. It was never said of the Seventh Ohio that it faltered in battle, that it failed to do its whole duty. You have been faithful, uncomplaining, and heroic. These things have not been accomplished without painful sacrifices. How painful, let the honorable scars many will carry to their graves answer. How painful, let this begrimed and tattered flag answer. How painful, these thinned ranks will answer. Your gallant colonel and lieutenant-colonel came home before you. Not as we could have wished them to come, but wearing the habiliments which all must wear; and now they lie yonder, and their graves are still wet with the tears of their mourning countrymen.

"Not so fortunate many of your countrymen, for they lie in unknown seclusion, but not in unhonored graves. We will not mourn these dead as those who die without hope, for their names shall be honored, so long as liberty is prized among men.

"'Death makes no conquest of these conquerors,
For now they live in fame, though not in life.'

"It is an honor to be engaged in this conflict, which those who share it should fully prize; and those who have been engaged in it have shown a self-sacrificing devotion to duty, seldom excelled. It is a conflict in favor of liberty against treason and traitors; against a desperate and implacable foe, fighting with desperate energy, that fraud, oppression, and crime may stalk abroad in daylight.

"Let us hope that the final overthrow of rebellion is at hand; that soon our soldiers may all return home, with—

"'Brows bound with victorious wreaths,
Their bruised arms hung up for monuments,
Their stern alarums changed to merry meetings,
Their dreadful marches to delightful measures.'

"On concluding, Mr. Grannis introduced Governor Brough, who also addressed the regiment. He said in substance as follows:

"Men of the Seventh Ohio—I know you are anxious to turn from this public to private greetings, to clasp friends and acquaintances in your hands and hearts. Under these circumstances I have not the courage to detain you. I will not read the glorious record of your achievements, for it would keep you so long. It is not necessary. We know your record in all its glory, but not, like you, in all its pain. A little over three years ago, on a Sabbath morning, you left Cleveland. Now, on a Sabbath morning, you return to us. That Sabbath was hallowed, by the purpose with which you went forth. This Sabbath is rendered sacred, by the joy with which you are welcomed back to us.

"On behalf of the State, I am here to give you a cordial greeting on your return. For the people of Cleveland, no formal greeting is necessary. In the crowd that gather around you, you can read the cordial welcome, that needs no words to express it.

"The Spartan mother, who sent her son to battle, bade him to return with his shield in honor, or on his shield in death. You have returned with your shields, and with honor reflected from them on you. But let us not forget that many have come home on their shields. We cannot forget those that, on another Sabbath morning, came home, and were received by the city in the weeds of mourning.

"We welcome you back, not only because you are back, but because you have reflected honor on your State. Standing, as I do, in the position of father of all of the regiments of the State, it will not do for me to discriminate; but I will say, that no regiment has returned to the bosom of the State, and none remains to come after it, that will bring back a more glorious record than the gallant old Seventh.

"There is no need to tell you what the lesson of this war is. You have learned it in many a weary march, and on many a field of carnage. None know better than you, that there are but two ways possible for the termination of this war. One is an inglorious peace and disgraceful submission, and the other is to completely crush the military power of the rebellion. There is no other way; and he who goes about on street-corners, and talks about a peace short of one or the other of these alternatives, is either grossly ignorant or intentionally attempting to deceive. More than that, no one knows better than yourselves, that to secure a lasting peace, when the military power of the rebellion is crushed, the cause of this infernal rebellion itself must be thoroughly wiped out. You have been taught that in many a fiery lesson, and know it to be a truth.

"There are gallant men and brave generals in the army laboring to reach this end; and we have confidence that their efforts will be crowned with success. God grant that it may be so. I had almost said that God and Grant will make it so.

"But I will detain you no longer. There is another greeting awaiting you in your homes—a greeting that no other eyes should witness. To that sacred and precious greeting I remit you."

The regiment now marched off to Camp Cleveland, escorted by the old members of the Seventh.

The men were given a brief furlough, after which preparations were made to be mustered out.

On the 4th of July, a grand ovation was given to the regiment, in connection with the Eighth Ohio; in fact, while the regiment remained in Cleveland, it was one continued ovation. The citizens vied with each other, in caring for and honoring the old Seventh. It seemed as if they could not do enough. These brave men will not soon forget the anxious care bestowed upon them by the citizens of Cleveland, during this closing period of their career in the service of their country.

After remaining for a brief period in camp, the regiment was mustered out; and after kindly farewells had been exchanged, each member departed for his home, from which he had been so long absent in protecting a Government that he loved from the ruthless touch of treason and slavery.

When the regiment entered the field, it numbered more than a thousand men. As these began to dwindle away by the shock of battle and the ravages of disease, new members came in, until we find nearly fourteen hundred men on the rolls, exclusive of three months' men: the latter would swell the number to about eighteen hundred men. Of the former, over six hundred were killed and wounded —the killed alone amounting to about one hundred and thirty. One hundred and upwards died from disease; while more than six hundred were discharged on account of disability arising from various causes. Many of those who were on the rolls at the time the regiment was mustered out were disabled for life, and were only retained for the want of an opportunity to be discharged. The whole number of able-bodied officers and men returning with the regiment was only two hundred and forty-five, leaving upwards of eleven hundred dead and disabled.

BIOGRAPHICAL SKETCHES.
BRIGADIER-GENERAL E. B. TYLER.[3]

E. B. Tyler entered the service as colonel of the Seventh. He brought with him some little military experience, having been a brigadier-general of militia before the rebellion broke out.

When General McClellan was about to make his advance into Western Virginia, he selected Tyler to lead the way, on account of his thorough acquaintance with that wild region, he having been engaged in purchasing furs from the people for many years. During the entire summer he was kept well out to the front. He was finally given a brigade, with which to assist General Cox in driving General Wise from the valley. He moved as far as Somerville, in the very heart of the enemy's country, and was soon after in the skirmish of Cross Lanes. From this time, during the remainder of his stay in the department, he was in command at Charleston, in the Kanawha Valley. In the winter following, he was ordered to Kelley's department, where he was again given a brigade, with which he did good service on the outposts. We next find him at the battle of Winchester, where he commanded a brigade. It was his command that charged the battery, for which it acquired so much renown. His conduct at this battle won him a star. He now served with his command in the Valley, accompanying it to the Rappahannock and back. After which he commanded the forces in the battle of Port Republic. His conduct in this engagement is above criticism. No general could have made better dispositions than he, and no one would have met with better success. Defeat was certain; and all that the best generalship could do, was to save barely a remnant of the command. It is a wonder that any artillery was saved. He gained much reputation in his command for the manner in which he acquitted himself in this battle. He soon after left his old brigade, and finally took command of a Pennsylvania brigade, which he led in the battle of Fredericksburg, in December, 1862. He had acquired a fine reputation with Governor Curtin, and his conduct in this battle confirmed it. The spring following he was assigned to a command in Baltimore, under General Schenck. At the time of the raid on Washington, in the summer of 1864, he was at the front. During an engagement he became separated from his command, and only escaped by dint of hard riding. After remaining concealed for some days, he escaped, and returned in safety to our lines. After this campaign he returned to Baltimore, where he is at the present time stationed.

BREVET BRIG.-GEN. J. S. CASEMENT.

J. S. Casement came into the regiment as major, and was just the man for the place. The regiment needed a practical, common-sense sort of a man, and it found him in the person of Jack Casement. Many of his previous years had been spent in the construction of railroads. In this he had not a superior in the United States. He is of small stature, but of iron frame; and for endurance has few equals. He will shoulder and walk off under a load that would make the most athletic tremble. He has probably superintended the laying of as much track as any man of his age.

On joining the regiment, the major at once made himself useful in looking after matters for the comfort of the command, that really belonged to no one to look to, and yet, when attended to, went far to improve the condition of the men. He rapidly acquired a knowledge of military tactics, which was afterwards to fit him for a leader. This was not difficult for him to do, for he made it a practical study. He was always on duty when the occasion required it. This habit of promptness he acquired while working large parties of men, and it never left him during his service. During the long marches in Western Virginia, he was ever watchful as to how matters were going on in the rear; and while other mounted officers were riding leisurely along, he was ever watchful of the train, as well as all other matters connected with the easy movement of the command. Arriving in camp, he made it his business to see that all was snug. At the affair at Cross Lanes he conducted himself with such gallantry as to endear him to the entire regiment. He rode over that fatal field as calm and collected as on drill. When his superior officers had escaped, he organized the balance of the command, and then commenced that memorable march over the hills and mountains, through the valleys and over the streams, of that wild waste. It was finally crowned with success, and the regiment felt proud of its major; and the Western Reserve felt proud, too, that they had sent so brave a man to serve with so brave a regiment. He now did his duty, until we find the regiment in the East, and in its expedition to Blue's Gap, Major Casement at its head. Just before reaching the fortifications, he made a speech. Said he: "Boys, you've not got much of a daddy, but with such as you have, I want you to go for those rebels." And they did go for them in earnest. It seems the boys did not object to the character of the "daddy." He now went with the regiment to Winchester, where he was engaged in that battle. He sat on his horse where the bullets were flying thickest, and seemed to be a stranger to fear. When the battle was nearly over, followed by a few men, he took possession of a piece of artillery, and held it until the close of the action. In the evening succeeding the battle, he found that ten rifle-bullets had passed through the cape of his coat on the left side, near to his arm.

Major Casement accompanied the regiment on its march up the Valley, making himself useful in the way of constructing bridges and roads. On arriving at Falmouth, on the Rappahannock, he tendered his resignation, which being accepted, he returned to his home. All missed the merry laugh, as well as the merry jokes, of the ever happy major.

He was not long permitted to enjoy home, however, as in the following summer he was made colonel of the One Hundred and Third Ohio Regiment, and immediately after left for the field. His regiment was ordered to Kentucky, in which department he served until Sherman's triumphant march on Atlanta, when he joined him, and soon after commanded a brigade. In this campaign he distinguished himself. After Sherman left for Savannah, Casement commanded a brigade in Thomas' army. At the battle of Franklin, which followed, he conducted himself in such a brilliant manner as to win a star by brevet. He now took part in the pursuit of the disorganized forces of Hood, and when it ceased, went to Wilmington, North Carolina, with the corps of General Schofield, where he has since remained.

The career of this dashing officer has been one of usefulness, and his numerous friends, as well as the entire country, appreciate his services.

BRIGADIER JOHN W. SPRAGUE.[4]

General Sprague entered the service as captain of Company E. He immediately gained a high character as an officer, both for his fine military bearing and gentlemanly deportment. His company was first in discipline, and during the time he was in command not one of his men was under arrest. His influence was such, that they seldom disobeyed an order. They regarded their captain as a fit person to lead them—one whose example was worthy of imitation.

During the trying marches in Western Virginia, Captain Sprague was ever at his post to encourage and cheer his men. A few days previous to the Cross Lanes affair, he was given a leave of absence; and soon after leaving for his home, he was taken prisoner by the enemy's cavalry. He remained in prison about a year, suffering all the hardships that the imagination can picture. When he was released, his hair had become gray, and his every appearance was indicative of great suffering. On his return, he was immediately commissioned colonel of the Sixty-third Ohio Regiment, and very soon after entered the field. From this time on he did gallant service in the armies of the West. His great military talent was at last acknowledged, and his vast services rewarded by conferring on him a star. He is now serving in the West.

LIEUT.-COL. SAMUEL McCLELLAND.

The subject of this sketch is a native of Ireland. He was born in 1829. While in his youth, his parents emigrated to this country, landing at Philadelphia, from whence they went to Pittsburgh. Remaining here for a short time, they removed to Youngstown, Ohio, where they have since resided.

He entered the service as first-lieutenant of Company I, and was at once active in the discharge of his duty. He accompanied the regiment to Western Virginia, where he took part in all the hard marches that followed. At the affair of Cross Lanes, he demonstrated, by his gallantry, the fact of the possession of great military talent; for he was brave, prudent, and skilful. Up to the battle of Winchester, he was with the regiment in every march and skirmish. At this battle he commanded a company, and had the honor of opening the battle, and sustaining it for a few minutes, till other companies formed on his flanks.

He was engaged in the following battles and skirmishes, which embrace every one in which the regiment was engaged: Cross Lanes, Winchester, Port Republic, Cedar Mountain, Antietam, Dumfries, Chancellorsville, Gettysburg, Lookout Mountain, Mission Ridge, and Taylor's Ridge. The various skirmishes and battles during the march of Sherman to Marietta, are to be added to this list. At the battle of Winchester he was slightly wounded in the head, but remained on the field, against the urgent solicitations of his friends, until the close of the engagement. At the battle of Taylor's Ridge he was severely wounded in the leg. He now returned to his home, but remained but a short time, rejoining his command before he was entirely recovered.

While in the East he was made captain of Company H, and after the battle of Taylor's Ridge, lieutenant-colonel. He now took command of the regiment; leading it through the arduous campaign of Sherman, as far as Marietta, in which service he won a fine reputation for ability as an officer. He was known and recognized throughout the army as the fighting colonel. At the above place, the old Seventh turned its steps homeward, commanded by Colonel McClelland, who had the proud satisfaction of leading the regiment into Cleveland, to do which the lamented Creighton was ever ambitious.

When encamped in the city, he set himself industriously at work preparing the regiment to be mustered out; which was done in due time.

McClelland was one of the few officers who were ever at their post. He was brave, active, and zealous, a good officer in every particular. His kindness and good feeling towards his fellow-soldiers won him many friends. His family have suffered severe loss, two brave brothers having died in battle. During all this affliction he has remained true to his country, his patriotism never growing cold for a moment.

MAJOR FREDERICK A. SEYMOUR.

The subject of this sketch came into the regiment as captain of Company G, having organized the company immediately after the first call for troops. He had seen a good deal of service in the militia of his native State, which was of great assistance to him in this new position. When the regiment was organized for the three-years' service, he was elected to his old position, which was an indication of the esteem his company had for him.

During the terrible campaign among the mountains of Western Virginia, his health became very much impaired; till just previous to the affair at Cross Lanes, he was compelled to leave his command and seek to restore it in his home. Therefore he was not in that skirmish. He soon after returned, but after reaching the Shenandoah Valley his health again failed him, and he once more sought to restore it by returning to his home. While he was absent the battle of Winchester was fought, and he therefore did not take part in the engagement.

He now accompanied the regiment in its march up the Shenandoah River, across the Blue Ridge, and back again to Front Royal; and from thence to Port Republic. In the battle fought at the latter place he was conspicuous for bravery. During that well-contested action be contributed all that lay in his power towards winning a victory. But valor alone cannot win a battle; numbers combined with it can only accomplish that. This was his first experience under fire; but he stood up to the work like a veteran; being second to none in deeds of daring.

Soon after this action he was engaged in the battle of Cedar Mountain, where he more than sustained the reputation acquired at Port Republic. This was a terrible battle, and every officer and private who fought there became a hero.

From this time forward the writer has no knowledge of his services, beyond the fact that he was promoted to major; which position he filled till some time in the fall of 1863, when he resigned, and returned to his home. It can be truly said that, wherever Major Seymour was placed, he endeavored to do his duty. Among his fellow-soldiers he had many friends, and he will always be remembered as a kind-hearted gentleman.

SURGEON FRANCIS SALTER.

Francis Salter entered the service as assistant surgeon of the Seventh Regiment; and on the resignation of Surgeon Cushing, was appointed surgeon. He held this position until the latter part of 1862, when he was made a medical director, and assigned to the staff of General Crooks. As a surgeon, he hardly had a superior in the service. His services were of great value in the hospitals, as he had had a long experience in those of England, his native country. He has remained in the service from the beginning of the war; and during that long period has alleviated the suffering of many a soldier.

C. J. BELLOWS.

The subject of this sketch was appointed surgeon of the regiment, from the position of assistant in the Fifth Ohio. Before entering the service he was enjoying a good practice in Northern Ohio, in which he had acquired a good reputation. While with the regiment he was much esteemed, by reason of his ability as a surgeon, as well as for his kind and courteous behavior.

G. E. DENIG.

On the appointment of Francis Salter to the post of surgeon, the subject of this sketch was made assistant. While with the regiment he was attentive to his duties, and always kind and obliging to those seeking medical aid. He many times acted as surgeon of the regiment; and on such occasions was always prompt in the discharge of his duty.

FREDERICK T. BROWN, D.D.

The subject of this sketch was born in Coshocton County, Ohio, of respectable and pious parents. His father was a wealthy merchant, and therefore gave his son a liberal education. After arriving at a proper age, he was sent to Princeton College, New Jersey, where he graduated. He early developed those Christian qualities which he has possessed in such an eminent degree during the whole course of his life. He was born to be a minister. At an early age his mind took a lasting hold upon religious truths; and it has never relaxed its energies in that direction for a single moment. He has gone on doing good from a child, his usefulness only increasing as his mind developed its powers. He has been a close student of theology during his whole life; and it is doing no discredit to others to say, that in this respect he has hardly a peer in the United States. He graduated at the Theological Seminaries at Princeton, New Jersey, and Geneva, Switzerland.

The Westminster Church, of Cleveland, Ohio, was organized by him; and in the course of his nine years' labor with it, increased from a small congregation to one of the most respectable religious societies of the city. He was pastor of this church at the breaking out of the rebellion.

While the Seventh Regiment was at Camp Dennison, he paid it a visit by request of some of the officers, and was immediately chosen its chaplain, there being but few dissenting voices. Immediately returning to his home, he tendered his resignation to his church, which, however, was not accepted; but in its stead, he was voted a leave of absence, which he accepted, but refusing to draw pay during the time. He joined the regiment early in July, while it was in Western Virginia, and at once entered upon his duties.

While here, he preached a sermon in one of the churches—to the rebel as well as Union people of the town—which was noted for the powerful arguments used against the position occupied by the South in relation to the Federal Government. This effort made him many friends in the village. He afterwards had a large influence over its people, being often invited to their homes. On such occasions he was received with a hearty welcome; although he never neglected an opportunity to reprove them for the opinions cherished by them.

While at Glenville, Gilmer County, he carried a message to General Cox, whose forces were somewhere on the banks of the Kanawha River. This has already been mentioned; but as it was an enterprise attended with much danger, we here copy a detailed account of it.

About the 15th day of July, Colonel Tyler, feeling it important to open communication with General Cox's forces on the Kanawha, determined to send a messenger with unwritten dispatches across the country through the enemy's lines; and as our chaplain could more readily be spared than any other member of the regiment deemed fitting to undertake the enterprise, the expedition was proposed to him. He accepted it willingly, though well aware of its difficulties and dangers. Colonel Tyler suggested to him to go in the character of a merchant or trader, so that, if arrested by roving guerillas or any of Wise's patrols, he could say he was on business to Gauley Bridge, or some other place. But he declined adopting the suggestion, as involving a possible lie, and asked to be left to his own resources.

Hastily divesting himself of every tell-tale mark of name, residence, or connection with the service, mounted on a blooded mare, captured from some guerrillas a few days before, and taking no rations but a bunch of cigars, an hour after receiving the order he started. It was a ride of a hundred and twenty miles through the enemy's country, by highways, and by-ways, and no ways at all, nearly half of it at night, sometimes alone, full of adventures, amusing and otherwise, and involving some narrow escapes from the enemy, but completely successful.

On the morning of the third day, at daylight, he struck the Kanawha, four miles below the mouth of the Pocotaligo; and there, for the first time, got word of General Cox, and learned that his camp was only four miles up the river. It was Sunday morning. He was soon at the general's quarters, and in the language of the chaplain himself, "received such a welcome as that genial man and accomplished Christian gentleman knows how to give." General Cox refused permission to him to return to us by the way he had come. He therefore remained with the general for the time; was with him at the capture of Charleston, and in the pursuit of Wise to Gauley Bridge, from whence he joined us again. Surviving members of the old Seventh will remember "the three times-three" cheers of each company in succession, as the chaplain rode along the line. We were on the march, a long distance from where he had left us, had not heard a word from him or of him, and had thought him lost; his arrival, safe and sound, coming from the direction of the enemy, was as one from the dead, or from Richmond.

At the battle of Cross Lanes he bore a gallant part, remaining with the command during the entire affair, and leaving only when all hope of saving the day had expired. He escaped, with others, through a gap in the enemy's lines, caused by well-directed volleys of musketry from the regiment. The same day he came into Gauley Bridge, after having rendered much service in bringing off the wagon-train. He soon after visited Cross Lanes, under a flag of truce, for the purpose of looking after our killed and wounded, as well as to learn the fate of those taken prisoners. While within the enemy's lines, he was treated civilly, but was refused the privilege of administering to the wounded, as well as visiting the prisoners. He therefore returned, without having accomplished, in the least degree, the object of his visit. The chaplain was soon after ordered to Charleston, where the scattered members of the Seventh had been collected.

While at this place he formed an agreeable acquaintance with many gentlemen of learning and ability, at whose houses he was a frequent visitor; and it may be truly said that on such occasions he added much to the fund of enjoyment.

While the regiment was at Charleston, a misunderstanding arose between the chaplain and Colonel Tyler, by reason of which the former felt it his duty to resign. His resignation was in due time accepted, and he was honorably mustered out of the service; the esteem and regrets of the entire command going with him to his home. While with the regiment his conduct had been above suspicion, and his sudden departure caused universal gloom.

Shortly after returning to his home in Cleveland, he was called to be pastor of a church at Georgetown, District of Columbia, which is both large and influential.

Not forgetting the cause of his country and her suffering soldiery, he is now engaged, in addition to his pastoral labors, in attending to the wants of the sick and wounded soldiers at the various hospitals in the vicinity of his home. Many a poor soldier of the republic will remember the words of consolation which have fallen on his ear from the lips of this devoted Christian.

In the personal appearance of Chaplain Brown, alone, there is a character. His light, fragile figure, erect and graceful carriage, strikes one as peculiarly fitting to his elegant, chaste, and mature intellect. He leaves an impression on the mind as lasting as it is positive. In his company the dark moments are lighted up. Generous and manly, he would distribute even his happiness among his fellows, were it possible. There are few men more companionable than he; and few ever won the love of their fellow-men equal to him. Endowed with rare conversational powers and a pleasing address, he always commands the attention of those around him. In public speaking, the first impression he makes upon the mind of the hearer is not such as would lead him to expect a flowery discourse; but as the speaker proceeds, it becomes evident that dry logic is not his only gift. His life is a constant reflection of truth. He takes a great grasp on eternal things; and lives greatly by seeking, as the one high aim of his studies, his labors, and his prayers, the supreme glory of God in the everlasting welfare of man. May such samples of Christian character be multiplied, till all the world has learned how great is God, and how great is goodness.

CHAPLAIN D. C. WRIGHT.

D. C. Wright was appointed chaplain during the winter of 1861. He reported to the regiment at Patterson's Creek, Virginia.

He was with the regiment at the battle of Winchester, where he rendered much assistance in caring for the wounded. He now followed the fortunes of the Seventh until its arrival at Port Republic, at which battle he served as aid to General Tyler. During the entire engagement he was much exposed, carrying dispatches in the most gallant style to different parts of the field. He was mentioned in the official reports for gallant conduct. After this battle he left for his home, and finally sent in his resignation, which was duly accepted.

Before the war broke out he was a minister of the Methodist Church, and acquired no little reputation as a revivalist preacher.

LIEUT.-COL. GILES W. SHURTLIFF.[5]

At the beginning of the rebellion, Giles W. Shurtliff was one of the teachers in the college at Oberlin. Immediately after the bombardment and capture of Fort Sumter, he organized a company, principally from among his pupils, and reported at Camp Taylor. He was with the regiment in its toilsome marches in Western Virginia, during which he was always at his post. During the affair at Cross Lanes he was taken prisoner, and now began those terrible hardships which no pen can describe, nor imagination picture. Prison life is a sort of living death,—a state of abeyance, where the mind is thrown back upon itself; where time, although passing, seems to stop, and the great world outside, to stand still. Through all this trial, and hardship, and misery, Colonel Shurtliff passed, without weakening his faith or his patriotism. He returned to his home, after more than a year's imprisonment, as firm in the support of the Government as ever. After allowing himself a short rest, he served in the Army of the Potomac on staff-duty; but was soon after made lieutenant-colonel of the Fifth United States Colored Infantry. He has since greatly distinguished himself in the numerous battles in the vicinity of Richmond. He is at the present time at his post, where he will probably remain until the rebellion is crushed, and the Government vindicated.

COLONEL ARTHUR T. WILCOX.

Arthur T. Wilcox is a native of Ohio, and entered the service as second-lieutenant of Company E. On the organization of the regiment for the three years' service, he was made a first-lieutenant, and assigned to the same company. He served with much credit in Western Virginia, until the Cross Lanes affair, when he was taken prisoner. He remained within the prison-walls of the enemy for more than a year, most of the time in Charleston, South Carolina, suffering every hardship; but coming out as true and pure a patriot as when he went in, he again joined his regiment, and was soon after made a captain. He now took part in all the battles of the West, in which the regiment was engaged,—Lookout Mountain, Mission Ridge, Ringgold, and Sherman's battles in the march on Atlanta. He came home with the regiment, and was in due time mustered out. He was not, however, permitted to remain long at home, for, when new regiments were forming, he was made a colonel, and assigned to the One Hundred and Seventy-seventh Regiment. He soon after joined his command, and was almost immediately ordered to the front. He joined General Thomas' forces, then falling back before the forces of General Hood. Arriving at Franklin, he was engaged in the bloody battle fought there, and greatly distinguished himself. He soon after arrived at Nashville with the army. The rebel army immediately advanced; and the two armies stood face to face, at the same time gathering strength for a desperate conflict. The Union army was triumphant, and the rebel hosts were beaten and demoralized. In this battle, Colonel Wilcox gained new laurels. He now took part in the pursuit of the scattered forces of Hood.

Every one who has fallen in company with Colonel Wilcox, will remember him as a genial friend and true gentleman. He has made many friends in the army as well as at home. He has chosen the law as a profession, and when "this cruel war is over" the writer wishes him the success his many virtues and talents merit.

LIEUT.-COL. JAMES T. STERLING.

James T. Sterling entered the service as first-lieutenant of Captain De Villiers' company. On the organization of the regiment for the three years' service, he was made captain. While at Camp Dennison he labored diligently to perfect his command in both drill and discipline; and when it entered the field it was second to none, so far as these essentials were concerned.

While in Western Virginia, Captain Sterling was on many scouts, in which service he showed great skill and bravery. Such adventures were very much to his liking.

In the affair at Cross Lanes he won the respect of all those who were witness to his coolness and daring. During the march to Charleston he made a good account of himself, being one of the most active in his labors, and among the wisest in his opinions.

He now followed the regiment to the East, where he engaged in all the marches and skirmishes which took place. At the battle of Winchester he commanded two companies; leading them into the hottest fire like a veteran. During the entire action he stood on the hill urging the men forward, regardless of the great danger to which he himself was exposed. He came through the battle, however, without a scratch, but with some holes in his clothing.

He now took part in the long chase of Jackson up the Valley, and from thence to Fredericksburg and back again; but was not in the battle of Port Republic, his company having been detailed for headquarters guard.

Very soon after this engagement he was made lieutenant-colonel of the One Hundred and Third Regiment, at that time about to be raised in the vicinity of Cleveland. He soon after reported to this regiment and was assigned to duty. He went with it to the field; but, after a limited period, was assigned the position of inspector-general on the staff of General Cox. He filled this position with much credit to himself, until early in the year 1864, when he resigned and returned to his home in Cleveland.

Colonel Sterling, as an officer, was much esteemed. As a companion, he was much admired. His easy manners and agreeable conversation gathered about him many friends. Every one regretted his departure from the Seventh; he had been with it through so many trials and dangers, that he was closely identified with it. His company thought well of him, and, therefore, his unexpected departure caused many regrets.

COLONEL JOEL F. ASPER.

Joel F. Asper was born in Huntington, Adams County, Pennsylvania, on the 20th day of April, 1822. When he was but five years old his father removed to Farmington, Ohio, by the slow process of a four-horse team and Pennsylvania wagon. The county of Trumbull was then but sparsely settled.

Until eighteen years of age he assisted his father in clearing a farm, at the same time attending a district school in winter. This is all the school education he ever had; all other education being acquired by his own exertion and application to study out of school.

Having a passion for reading and writing, he was led to study law. But previous to this, however, he commenced teaching a school in Southington, but, for some reason, left it after one month's experience. Early in the year 1842, we find him in the law-office of Crowell and Abel, at Warren, Ohio, and working for his board at the American Hotel.

In 1843, he carried the Western Reserve Chronicle through several townships, and during the entire year did not miss a trip.

In August, 1844, he was admitted to the bar, but remained with General Crowell till 1845, when he learned the daguerrean business, but not succeeding in this, in October following opened a law-office at Warren. His first year's practice netted him over four hundred dollars, and it increased from year to year.

In 1846 be was elected a justice of the peace, and in the following year was married to Miss Elizabeth Brown.

In 1847 he was elected prosecuting attorney. In 1849, was announced as one of the editors of the Western Reserve Chronicle; and wrote, during the campaign of that year, all of the leading political articles published in its columns. During the summer of 1848, Mr. Parker, proprietor of the paper, left for a pleasure excursion, and while absent, Mr. Asper, being left in charge, took ground against General Taylor. During this campaign he did much towards developing anti-slavery sentiments in the party. For this conduct he was denounced by the minority of his party. At this time he made a speech before a Whig convention, which is said to have been the best effort of his life. Carrying out these sentiments, he sustained Martin Van Buren for the presidency, and in the following year ran for prosecuting attorney on the Free-Soil ticket, but was defeated.

In 1850 he moved to Chardon, Ohio, and edited a Free-Soil paper until 1852, when, it proving a losing business, he returned to Warren, where he again commenced the practice of the law, which he continued until the breaking out of the rebellion, in 1861. He was among the first in Northern Ohio to tender a company to the Governor. It marched to camp on the 25th of April. He served in the regiment until March, 1863, when he was honorably mustered out of the United States service. During this time he took part in the affair of Cross Lanes and the battle of Winchester, in which last engagement he was severely wounded. After the Cross Lanes affair he accompanied a detachment of four hundred men to Charleston, rendering much assistance during the march. He was promoted to lieutenant-colonel during his service with the regiment, in which position he commanded the regiment in the retreat of Pope's army from the Rapidan.

On returning to Warren he opened an office, and in August organized the Fifty-first Regiment National Guards, and was elected its colonel.

When, in the spring of 1864, the corps was ordered into the field, his regiment was among the first to move. It went to Johnson's Island, and while there the noted John H. Morgan commenced a raid through Kentucky. To resist him, several militia regiments were ordered to the front; among them was the Fifty-first, now become the One Hundred and Seventy-first.

Arriving at Cincinnati, he reported to General Hobson, and was ordered to Keller's Bridge by train. Soon after getting off the cars, it was attacked by the enemy in overwhelming numbers. After a gallant fight of six hours, the brave little band of heroes was compelled to surrender. No regiment of new troops ever did better: it made itself a name which history will perpetuate.

The regiment was mustered out on the 20th of August, 1864. Asper now perfected his arrangements to move to Missouri, which he put into execution in October following. He is now engaged in the practice of law at Chillicothe, in the above State.

MAJOR W. R. STERLING.

The subject of this sketch entered the service as Captain of Company I. He carried with him some considerable military experience, having been connected with a company in his native State. He accompanied the regiment in its Western Virginia campaign, taking an honorable part in the affair at Cross Lanes. He was with the detachment in its march over the mountains to Charleston, during which he rendered great assistance, contributing largely towards bringing the command off in safety.

From Charleston he returned to his home on leave, but soon after returned to his command, accompanied by a number of recruits. He now took part in the various marches and skirmishes occurring in the mountain department of Eastern Virginia. He was not in the battles of Winchester or Port Republic; but was in all the marches occurring before and after those engagements. At the battle of Cedar Mountain he did yeoman's service. His company was led with such coolness and bravery, that many a rebel was made to bite the dust. He now remained with the regiment until General Hooker came to the command of the Army of the Potomac, when Captain Sterling was assigned a position on his staff. In this capacity he served until after the battle of Chancellorsville. A short time after this engagement he was taken prisoner by a roving band of rebels, and conveyed to Richmond, where he was for some time confined in prison. He was finally taken further south to another prison, from which, in the summer of 1864, he escaped; and after spending some time in the mountains, during which he suffered many hardships, finally joined the Union forces in Tennessee.

He was a brave and competent officer. While on Hooker's staff he was promoted to major.

MAJOR E. J. KREIGER.

The subject of this sketch is a native of Germany, and entered the service as a sergeant in a company composed of his fellow-countrymen. He very soon rose to the rank of lieutenant, and before the term of service of the regiment expired, to that of captain. He was in the following battles and skirmishes: Cross Lanes, Winchester, Port Republic, Cedar Mountain, Antietam, Dumfries,

Chancellorsville, Gettysburg, Mission Ridge, Lookout Mountain, Ringgold, and in all the engagements in which his regiment took part in Sherman's march on Atlanta. No officer can show a prouder record. He was always with his command, and on all occasions showed great bravery and gallantry, as well as ability to command.

Immediately after the Seventh was mustered out, he was appointed major of the One Hundred and Seventy-seventh Regiment, and left soon after for the field. He now added to the above glorious list of battles that of Franklin, where he fully sustained the honors that he gained while with the old Seventh. He is at the present time in General Thomas' army, where he will remain, if his life is spared, until the overthrow of the rebellion.

CAPTAIN J. B. MOLYNEAUX.

The subject of this sketch was born, January 1, 1840, at Ann Arbor, in the State of Michigan. At the age of four years his father removed to Penn Yan, New York, and soon after to Bath and Elmira, in the same State. In 1854, young Molyneaux went to Belville, Ohio, and commenced the study of medicine in the office of Dr. Whitcomb. He remained for nearly a year, when, not liking the study, he went to Cleveland, Ohio, and entered the job-office of John Williston, where he learned the art of printing.

Having a natural liking for military life, he joined the Light Guards, and afterwards the Sprague Cadets, of which he was appointed drill-master. On the first call for troops, he joined a company being raised by Captain De Villiers, as a private, being among the first to enroll his name. Soon after arriving in camp, he was appointed a sergeant, and, immediately after, drill-master for the non-commissioned officers of the regiment. On the three years' organization, he was unanimously chosen first-lieutenant by the vote of his company. He remained with this company during the earlier part of the campaign in Western Virginia, taking a gallant part in the affair of Cross Lanes, as also in the final march of Major Casement's detachment to Charleston. After this action, he was placed in command of Company E, which command he held until January, 1862, and then being relieved, only for the purpose of receiving the appointment of adjutant.

He took part in all the marches and skirmishes in both Western and Eastern Virginia. At the battle of Winchester, he was mentioned, in the official report of his colonel, for gallantry on the battle-field. At the battle of Port Republic, he won new laurels, being constantly under the enemy's fire. In the fearful struggle at Cedar Mountain, he particularly distinguished himself. He was, for a limited time, in command of the regiment, during which he extricated it from a position, where, under a less skilful leader, it would have been captured. In this gallant exploit, Molyneaux lost two horses, one of them being pierced by fourteen bullets.

In September, 1862, he was appointed captain, after having waived rank three times. This position he held until March, 1863, when, on account of wounds and ill-health, he was compelled to resign. In the mean time, he was with the regiment in all its marches, as well as the battle of Antietam and the affair at Dumfries.

On his return home he followed his occupation of a printer, until the governor's call for the National Guard, when he again entered the service as a captain. His regiment being stationed in the defences of Washington, he was placed in command of a fort, which was, a part of the time, garrisoned by several companies. After the expiration of his term of service, he returned to his home in Cleveland, and resumed his business.

CAPTAIN CHARLES A. WEED.

Charles A. Weed was born, March 30, 1840, in Lake County, Ohio. He enlisted in Captain John N. Dyer's company, on the 22d day of April, 1861. After its arrival in camp, he was made orderly-sergeant, in which capacity he developed fine military talent, such as led his company, at an early time, to look upon him as a proper person for promotion when a vacancy should occur. Therefore, on the final organization of the company for the three years' service, he was made a first-lieutenant. He was with the regiment during the entire Western Virginia campaign, taking part in the skirmish at Cross Lanes, in which he took command of the company after the death of Captain Dyer, which position he held until January, 1862, when he was relieved by an officer promoted to the captaincy by reason of superiority of rank. He was soon after made captain, February 5, 1862, and assigned to Company E.

He now took part in all the marches and skirmishes in Eastern Virginia, and also in the battle of Winchester, where he displayed great gallantry. After this battle, he commanded his company in the pursuit of Jackson to Harrisonburg, and in the toilsome march to Fredericksburg, and the return to Front Royal. He was now in the advance to Port Republic. In the battle which succeeded, he displayed great courage, as well as ability to command. He took part in the battle of Cedar Mountain and Antietam, and also in the skirmish at Dumfries. On the 22d of February, 1863, he resigned, and returned to his home.

There were few better officers in the regiment. He was prompt in the discharge of his duty, seldom questioning the propriety of an order emanating from a superior, but executing it at once. In his intercourse with his fellow-soldiers, he was frank and courteous, and all cherished the kindest feelings towards him.

CAPTAIN JUDSON N. CROSS.

The subject of this sketch is a native of Ohio. When the war broke out he was attending college at Oberlin, Ohio. He immediately enrolled himself in Captain Shurtliff's company, and was soon after made a first-lieutenant. He served with his company in Western Virginia, with much credit to himself and profit to his country. At the skirmish of Cross Lanes he was brave, and showed that he was competent to command. During the affair, he was severely wounded in the arm and taken prisoner. At the battle of Carnifex Ferry, which followed soon after, he was recaptured by the forces under General Rosecrans. Being unfit for service, he now went to his home, where it was thought he might recover sufficiently to rejoin his command. But after the expiration of some months, being still unable for service, he was ordered on recruiting service at Cleveland, Ohio. He was engaged in this work until the fall of 1862, when he was honorably mustered out of the service, on account of the unimproved condition of his wound. In the mean time, however, he had been promoted to a captaincy.

CAPTAIN JOHN F. SCHUTTE.

Entered the service as a lieutenant in Captain Wiseman's company, and on its organization for three years, was made its captain. He was with the regiment until just before its affair at Cross Lands, when, being on picket duty on the banks of the Gauley River, he imprudently crossed over, and after advancing some miles into the enemy's country, was fired upon by a body of cavalry, concealed in the bushes, and mortally wounded. After being taken to an old building close by, he was left, at his own request, and soon after expired. The rebels buried him on the spot. No braver officer ever entered the service. Had he lived, he would undoubtedly have distinguished himself.

At the time of his death, no officer had a better reputation. His company was somewhat difficult to manage, but while he was in command, it was not surpassed for discipline, and hardly equalled. He was kind to every one who did his duty, but when one of his men failed to do that, he came down upon him with a heavy hand.

His loss was deeply felt throughout the entire command. His company had recognized in him a leader, and they deplored his loss.

LIEUT. LOUIS G. DE FOREST.

Louis G. De Forest was born in Cleveland, Ohio, on the 9th of September, 1838. His youth was spent in the city schools, where he acquired a fair education. In 1853, at the age of fifteen years, he entered the store of N. E. Crittenden. It is a high compliment to his industry and business habits, that he has remained in his employ since that date, with the exception of the time that he spent in the military service.

Having a natural taste for military life, in 1859 he joined a company of Light Guards as a private, but soon rose to the positions of corporal, sergeant, and finally lieutenant. The latter position he filled with credit, until the rebellion broke out, when, on the organization of the Sprague Cadets, for three months' service, he hastened to enroll his name. He was soon made orderly sergeant, which position he held when the company went into camp. After the regiment arrived in Camp Dennison, he was elected a second-lieutenant of his company. And on its final organization for the three years' service, he was chosen its adjutant, by a vote of its officers, and soon after received his commission, with the rank of first-lieutenant.

He accompanied the regiment in its arduous Western Virginia campaign, and during the time Colonel Tyler commanded a brigade, he served as acting assistant adjutant-general. At the affair at Cross Lanes, he took a prominent as well as gallant part. He was among the number of those who made the march over the mountains to Elk River and Charleston.

He accompanied the regiment to Kelly's department, where he again acted as acting assistant adjutant-general to Colonel Tyler, serving in this capacity until his resignation, which took place in March.

When the National Guard was organized, he raised a company, and was made its captain. In this position he served during the one hundred days' campaign of this corps, being stationed in a fort in the vicinity of Washington.

Every one who came in connection with the Seventh Regiment will remember the stentorian voice and soldierly bearing of its first adjutant.

LIEUTENANT HALBERT B. CASE.

Halbert B. Case was born in Trumbull County, Ohio, May 3, 1838. His father being a farmer, he was bred to that occupation. At the age of sixteen years he entered the W. R. Seminary, at Farmington, Ohio, preparatory to entering college. After a year and a half spent in this institution of learning, he went to Oberlin, where he pursued his studies for more than three years, when, his health failing him, he was compelled to leave college.

During the winter of 1859, his health being somewhat improved, he went to Tiffin, Ohio, and commenced the study of the law. He remained here two winters. In the spring of 1860, being in indifferent health, he returned to his home in Mecca, Ohio, where he pursued his studies privately for some months. After which he went to Warren, and studied law with Forrist and Burnett until the breaking out of the rebellion.

On the 19th day of April, 1861, deeming it his duty to serve his country, he enlisted in Asper's company, the first organized in the county. He was soon after made orderly-sergeant. When the three years' organization was made, he was unanimously chosen a lieutenant by a vote of his company.

He served honorably during the campaign in Western Virginia, taking an active part in the affair of Cross Lanes, sharing the fortunes of the detachment under Major Casement.

Among the first promotions that were made in November, 1861, he was remembered by the authorities, and appointed a first-lieutenant. He accompanied the regiment to Eastern Virginia, where he joined the expedition to Romney and Blue's Gap.

While at Patterson's Creek he felt it his duty to resign his commission, on account of a personal difficulty with Colonel Tyler. He therefore left the regiment early in February, with the regrets of the entire command.

He was not long permitted to remain at home, for his former services were acknowledged by giving him a commission as captain in the Eighty-fourth Regiment, which was being organized for three months' service. This position being accepted, he proceeded with his regiment to Cumberland, Maryland. Soon after its arrival he was made provost-marshal and commandant of the post. In this position he won an enviable reputation. Among his first orders was one against the use and sale of intoxicating liquors, which he proceeded to enforce in an effectual manner; and thus materially aided in maintaining order and quiet at the post.

After nearly five months' service, when the regiment was mustered out, he was appointed colonel, for the purpose of reorganizing it for three years' service. He immediately entered upon this task; but owing to the number of regiments at that time being organized in Northern Ohio, he was but partially successful. The regiment being finally consolidated with the One Hundred and Twenty-fourth Ohio, he returned to his home.

He soon after entered the law-school at Ann Arbor, Michigan; and after a year and a half spent at this university, he graduated, with the degree of L. L. B. Soon after, he returned home, married, and commenced the practice of his profession at Youngstown, Ohio.

LIEUTENANT HENRY Z. EATON.

Lieutenant Eaton entered the service as a private, but on the three years' organization was made a second-lieutenant. He was with the regiment constantly during the campaign in Western Virginia, and always at his post. He took an important part in the Cross Lanes affair, and in the march of Major Casement's detachment.

He now went to the East with the regiment, when Colonel Tyler being given a brigade, he was assigned to his staff as aid-de-camp. He held this position at the battle of Winchester; and no one in the army did better service. He was constantly in the saddle, riding fearlessly in the heat of the battle, a fair mark for the rebels. During the engagement his horse was wounded. He was mentioned in official reports for gallant conduct. He soon after took part in the battle of Port Republic, where he added much to his already well-earned reputation for courage and other soldierly qualities. He now followed the regiment to Alexandria, where he returned to his company and to the front of Pope's army, where he was at the battle of Cedar Mountain, in which he was severely wounded. He soon after returned to his home, and finally resigned, on account of disability from wounds.

LIEUTENANT A. H. DAY.

A. H. Day was a lieutenant in company F, in which capacity he accompanied the regiment in Western and Eastern Virginia, taking part in the battles of Winchester and Port Republic, in both of which he did good service. In the latter he was severely wounded in the shoulder, by reason of which he was soon after compelled to resign.

LIEUTENANT WILLIAM D. SHEPHERD.

William D. Shepherd entered the service as a private in company D. He was soon after made a sergeant, and at Camp Dennison, orderly. He followed the fortunes of his company through the wilds of Western Virginia till the affair at Cross Lanes, where he showed great gallantry. He went with his company to Charleston, where, in the absence of Lieutenant Weed, he took command. During this time the company was detailed to guard a party who were engaged in erecting a telegraph line from Point Pleasant to Gauley Bridge. In this service he gave good satisfaction to all concerned in the undertaking.

He now remained with his command until a few days before the battle of Winchester, when he was compelled to leave the field on account of inflammation in one of his eyes. It had become very painful long before he would consent to go to the rear. A fever soon following, he was completely prostrated. He now went to his home, where he was engaged in the recruiting service. He returned to his regiment late in the summer, and having been promoted to first-lieutenant, was immediately made adjutant. He served with the regiment in this capacity until after the affair at Dumfries, when he was compelled to resign on account of ill-health.

After his return home he did great service in recruiting. In the winter of 1863-4 he canvassed Lake and Geanga counties, and was the means of enlisting a large number of men. On these occasions he made speeches, of which any public speaker might well be proud.

In the fall of 1864 he raised a company for the National Guard, which he commanded in the one hundred days' service. Returning to his home, he was appointed a quartermaster, with the rank of captain, and assigned to a division in the Twenty-third Army Corps.

His promotion was won in the field, and therefore honorable. His commission as second-lieutenant bears the date of November 25th, 1861; and that of first-lieutenant early in the following year.

Every one who has fallen in company with Lieutenant Shepherd will remember him as a genial friend and profitable companion. His frankness and courtesy have made him many friends. To know him, is to esteem him. I doubt whether he has an enemy in the world. He has always been a warm supporter of the Government, although not an American citizen by birth, having been born in Canada.

LIEUTENANT E. HUDSON BAKER.

Lieutenant Baker entered the service in Company C. He remained with the regiment during its entire campaign in Western Virginia, doing good service. At the affair at Cross Lanes, he was particularly conspicuous for gallantry. He now took command of the company, which he held during the remainder of his term of service. He was in the battle of Winchester, where he commanded his company with great credit to himself. As an officer, he was very popular with his command; as a companion, he was sociable and benevolent. He was finally compelled to resign from ill-health, but much against his wishes. He desired to remain until the close of his regular term of service, and then return with his old comrades; but his increasing debility would not admit.

LIEUTENANT RALPH LOCKWOOD.

Lieutenant Ralph Lockwood entered the regiment, on its first organization, in Company E. He served creditably through the Western Virginia campaign, taking part in the skirmish at Cross Lanes, and the battles of Winchester and Port Republic. In these battles he was distinguished for personal courage. By constant exposure, he contracted a rheumatic difficulty, which finally compelled him to resign, at a time when his services were much needed in the regiment.

LIEUTENANT T. T. SWEENEY.

Lieutenant T. T. Sweeney entered the service in Company B. He saw much service in Western Virginia, and was in every respect a gallant officer. At Cross Lanes, he made an honorable record. Soon after this skirmish, he resigned his commission, and returned to his home in Cleveland, Ohio.

LIEUTENANT EDWARD W. FITCH.

Lieutenant Fitch entered the service in Company I. He served faithfully until after the skirmish of Cross Lanes, in which he bore a gallant part. While at Charleston, he resigned his commission, and returned to his home.

LIEUTENANT A. J. WILLIAMS.

Lieutenant Williams came into the regiment as second-lieutenant of Company D, which position he filled with much credit till after the affair at Cross Lanes, when he resigned his commission. At the time the above skirmish took place he was sick, and therefore did not take part in it. Previous to this he had toiled on with his company, through all its terrible marches and dreary bivouacks; and for this is entitled to the gratitude of the country.

OUR DEAD.

COLONEL WILLIAM R. CREIGHTON AND LIEUT.-COLONEL ORRIN J. CRANE.

Colonel William R. Creighton was born in Pittsburgh, Pennsylvania, in June, 1837. At the age of ten years, he entered a shoe-store, where he remained for two years; after which he entered a commercial college, where he remained for six months. But these pursuits were not to his liking—he had no taste for accounts. We next find him, at the age of thirteen years, in the job-office of McMillin, in Pittsburgh, where he remained for four years, completing his apprenticeship. The year following, he went to Cleveland, Ohio, and entered the Herald office, where he remained till the fall of 1860, with the exception of one winter spent in a job-office in Chicago.

He united with the fire companies of both Pittsburgh and Cleveland, and was an active and zealous member. In 1858, he joined the military organization known as the Cleveland Light Guards, and soon after became a sergeant, and a lieutenant. He advanced in rank without any effort—it was a matter of course.

When the rebellion broke out, his love of adventure would not permit him to remain at home; but he immediately set himself at work organizing a company, which was completed in a few days, and, on the 22d day of April, marched to Camp Taylor. He immediately commenced drilling his company, and with such success, that it took the lead of all then in camp.

At this time his military genius shone so conspicuously that he was looked on by all as the future leader of the regiment.

All will remember with what skill and pride he led the regiment in its first march. It was on a beautiful Sabbath morning; and as the young soldier, with a proud step, took his position at the head of the column, every eye was turned upon him in admiration; one could see in the countenances of the men, a willingness to follow such a leader amid the hail and thunder of battle. Before reaching Camp Dennison, this admiration warmed into a determination to place him in a position when, at no distant day, he could be made available as the commander of the regiment. Therefore, on its arrival at camp, he was elected lieutenant-colonel, a position which he did not seek, nor intimate to any that he desired. Very many were desirous of making him colonel.

During the stay of the regiment at Camp Dennison, he took no active part, seldom being seen on drill, or on duty of any kind. When the regiment was about leaving, however, he took command, Colonel Tyler having gone to Virginia in advance of the starting of the regiment. Previous to the movement, every thing had been arranged in perfect order; but this arrangement was partially defeated by the indecent haste of a captain. An unutterable look of scorn and contempt settled upon the features of Creighton; but not a word passed his lips. He never entirely forgave that officer for this act of disobedience of orders, till his death, when all feelings of animosity gave way to regrets for his loss; for, outside of a disposition to criticise the conduct of his superiors, he was a brave as well as competent officer.

Arriving at Clarksburg, he turned over the command to Colonel Tyler; but on arriving at Glenville, he again assumed command, which he held until reaching Cross Lanes; in the mean time, drilling the regiment daily when in camp. During this time it improved rapidly; in fact, it acquired, during this short interval, most of the proficiency it possessed.

On the march back to Cross Lanes from Twenty-mile Creek, he was with the advance, in command of the skirmishers. During the affair which succeeded, at the above place, he bore himself creditably. During the retreat, his horse fell with him: seizing the holsters, he started on foot through the underbrush, but soon after saw his horse coming after him at full speed. He again mounted; but in a short time his horse again fell, when, for the second time, he abandoned him; but he was soon joined by his faithful "Johnny," and this time the devoted horse carried its gallant rider safely to Gauley Bridge.

This misfortune to the regiment completely unmanned him. Meeting a comrade on the retreat, who was not in the engagement, he burst into tears, and, grasping his hand, in choked utterances related the story of their encounter.

While the regiment remained at Charleston, Creighton was in command, and was untiring in his efforts to advance his command in both drill and discipline; and I doubt whether any regiment in the field made more rapid progress towards perfection. It seemed to emulate its leader, who was ever at his post.

When an order came for five hundred picked men from the regiment to report to General Benham for duty, in the pursuit of Floyd, he was chosen to command the detachment. On arriving at Benham's headquarters, he was given the advance, and, for several days, was separated from Floyd's camp by a range of mountains only. He was finally given a brigade, although only a lieutenant-colonel, and ordered across a range of mountains to the rear of the enemy; but for some reason no attack was made, and soon after, half of the command was ordered back.

During the pursuit of Floyd, he travelled on foot at the head of his regiment. When the rebel army was likely to be overtaken, Benham remarked to him, that "he depended on him to rout the enemy," and gave him the post of honor; but when the firing became rapid, his regiment was ordered to the front, where a part of it was engaged in skirmishing, while the balance were smoking their pipes and engaging in sports, almost under the guns of the enemy, Creighton enjoying the fun as well as any in the command.

The detachment returned, after fifteen days' absence, without the loss of a man, save one injured by the accidental discharge of a gun.

The regiment now went to the East, where, soon after, Tyler was given a brigade, and Creighton again commanded the regiment.

At the battle of Winchester, which followed soon after, his was the first regiment in the famous charge of the Third brigade, for which it acquired such renown. He disagreed with the commanding officer as to the manner of making the charge, preferring to deploy before advancing, than to charge a battery in close column. But throwing all personal feelings and preferences aside, he dashed forward, and finally deployed his regiment within eighty yards of the enemy's line of battle, and under a terrible fire of both musketry and artillery. His horse being shot from under him, he seized a musket, and engaged in the strife, firing rapidly till near the close of the battle, when he was compelled to cease for the purpose of executing some order.

On the return of the command to New Market, after the pursuit of Jackson to near Harrisonburg, the company tents were ordered to be delivered up; whereupon Creighton was very indignant, and, in connection with other officers, sent in his resignation. They were ordered to report to General Shields the next morning. Accordingly, dressed in their "best," they reported. They were received with all the politeness that pompous general knew how to assume, with an invitation to be seated. The general informed them that their resignations would not be accepted; but remarked, that, "if they *desired* it, he would have their names stricken from the army rolls in disgrace." This witticism rather amused Creighton than otherwise, and he returned to camp with a much better opinion of the general than he was possessed of before making his visit.

He now commanded the regiment in its march to Fredericksburg, sharing with his men the hardships attending the toilsome march; and when, a few days after, the regiment returned to the Valley, he did much to cheer the men in that discouraging march.

At Front Royal he remained with his regiment during a heavy storm, to which it was exposed without tents, disdaining to seek shelter and comfort while his men were thus exposed.

The men were now very destitute of clothing, especially shoes; but when ordered, he moved to Columbia Bridge, followed by one hundred men barefooted. He now went personally to General Shields, but was coldly received by that general, being subjected to insulting remarks. He came back to his regiment with that same unutterable expression of contempt stamped upon his features, which all will remember who served with him in the field; and getting his men in column, closed in mass, made a speech. Said he: "I am unable to procure shoes or other comforts for you; but I will follow these generals until there is not a man left in the regiment. Forward, company H!" And he did follow them to Port Republic, where his words came near proving true.

At this battle his bravery and daring were observed by every one. He made repeated charges with his regiment, the line being as correct as on dress-parade. After one of these charges, the enemy's cavalry came dashing towards his regiment, and dispositions were immediately made for forming a square; but the enemy wisely wheeled, and charged another regiment. The colonel of this regiment, being unable to get his men in position, shouted in a stentorian voice: "Men of the ——th, look at the Seventh Ohio; and d—n you, weep!"

In this battle the regiment made five charges, under the leadership of Creighton; and each time driving the enemy.

After the battle was over, and the regiment on the retreat, seeing a wounded captain lying almost within the enemy's lines, he rode up to his company, and pointing to where he was lying, said: "Do you see your captain over yonder? *Now, go for him!*" They did go for him, and succeeded in bringing him from the field in safety.

Only a few were missing from the regiment in this action, although the list of killed and wounded was fearful.

We next find Creighton at the battle of Cedar Mountain, where a small division fought the whole of Jackson's army on ground of his own choosing. Creighton handled his regiment with a dexterity that told fearfully on the ranks of the enemy. He was finally severely wounded, and compelled to leave the field. In doing so, he kept his face to the foe, saying that "no rebel ever saw his back in battle; and never would." He was taken to Washington, where the bullet was extracted from his side, which was an exceedingly painful operation. Soon after this he came to his home; but while still carrying his arm in a sling, he reported to his regiment.

While at home the battle of Antietam was fought, which was the only one in which he failed to participate. Soon after his return, the affair at Dumfries occurred, where, through his ingenuity and skill, Hampton's cavalry command was defeated by a mere handful of men. For this he was publicly thanked by Generals Slocum and Geary.

He now took part in the battle of Chancellorsville, where he won new laurels. It is said that being ordered by General Hooker to fall back, he refused to do so until able to bring Knapp's Battery safely to the rear; for which disobedience of orders he was recommended for promotion. This battery was from his native city, and in it he had many friends.

Next he was at Gettysburg, where he fought with his accustomed valor.

We now find him at Lookout Mountain and Mission Ridge, in "Hooker's battle above the clouds," where the victory was so suddenly and unexpectedly won, that scarcely sufficient time intervened in which to display valor. It was simply a race for the top of the mountain on the part of our men; and a corresponding race on the part of the rebels for the foot of the mountain on the opposite side.

After this battle came the pursuit of Bragg. His rear-guard was overtaken at Ringgold, Georgia, where it was securely posted on the top of Taylor's Ridge—a naked eminence. It was madness to undertake to drive them from this hill, without the use of artillery to cover the assault; but in the excitement of the moment the order was given. In this assault Creighton commanded a brigade. Forming his command, he made a speech. "Boys," said he, "we are ordered to take that hill. I want to see you walk right up it." After this characteristic speech, he led his men up the hill. It soon became impossible to advance against the terrible fire by which they were met; he, therefore, led them into a ravine, but the rebels poured such a fire into it from all sides, that the command was driven back. Reaching a fence, Creighton stopped, and facing the foe, waited for his command to reach the opposite side. While in this position he fell, pierced through the body with a rifle bullet. His last words were: "Oh, my dear wife!" and he expired almost immediately. The brigade now fell rapidly back, carrying the remains of its idolized commander with it.

Lieutenant-Colonel Orrin J. Crane was born in Troy, New York, in the year 1829. At three years of age his parents moved to their native State, Vermont. Soon after, his father died, leaving but limited means for the support and education of his children. His mother was a Christian woman, and devoted to her children. From her he received his first lessons of life; and a worthy teacher he had. He cherished his mother with the utmost affection, dwelling upon her goodness with almost child-like simplicity. It was touching to listen to the words of love and confidence falling for her, from the lips of the sturdy warrior, who braved the battle-fire without a tremor.

In early youth he went to live with an uncle, and in about 1852 came with him to Conneaut, Ohio, where he employed himself in mechanical labor. He spent one year on the Isthmus, and after his return went to Cleveland, where he engaged in the occupation of a ship-carpenter, following this trade till the fall of Sumter. While in Cleveland he associated himself with a military organization.

He entered the service as first-lieutenant in Captain Creighton's company; and on his promotion, was made captain. He early devoted himself to the instruction of his company; and it can be said that it lost nothing of the efficiency it acquired under the leadership of Creighton.

After the regiment entered the field, his services were invaluable. I doubt if the entire army contains an officer who has performed more service, in the same length of time, than Crane. If a bridge was to be constructed, or a road repaired, he was sent for to superintend it. If the commissary department became reduced, he was the one to procure supplies. No undertaking was too arduous for his iron-will to brave. There was no fear of starvation while the sturdy Crane was present. All relied on him with the utmost confidence, and no one was ever disappointed in him.

At the affair of Cross Lanes, where he first came under fire, he was more than a hero; he seemed possessed of attributes of a higher nature. He moved amid that sheet of flame, as if possessed of a soul in communion with a higher power. He inspired his men with true courage. They stood like a wall, and fell back only when ordered by their leader, then dashed through the strong line of the enemy with a bravery which was truly sublime. The enemy, although five to one, hesitated, swayed backward, and finally fled, so severely punished, that for the time they did not pursue. In that long march, over the mountains to Gauley Bridge, he was still the proud leader.

After his arrival at the above place, he was sent out to the front, up New River, where he rendered valuable service.

He was in every march and skirmish in both Western and Eastern Virginia, until, we find the regiment at the battle of Winchester. In this engagement he showed the same indomitable and true courage. He held his men to the work of carnage so fearfully, that the enemy's slain almost equalled his command.

We now find him in every battle in which his regiment was engaged in the East. Port Republic, Cedar Mountain (where he was slightly wounded), Antietam, Dumfries, Chancellorsville, and Gettysburg. In all of these he *led* his command, and the dead of the enemy left on the field before it attest how well he led it.

At the battle of Antietam, he commanded the regiment, and during the latter part of the engagement, a brigade.

Before the regiment left for the West, he was made lieutenant-colonel; a position which his ability and long, as well as faithful, service of his country rendered him eminently qualified to fill.

Arriving in the West, he commanded the regiment in the battles of Lookout Mountain and Mission Ridge, where he added new laurels to his already imperishable name. At fatal Ringgold, he again commanded the regiment. He led it up the steep ascent, where the whistling of bullets made the air musical; and where men dropped so quietly that they were scarcely missed, except in the thinned ranks of the command. The regiment had not recovered from the shock produced by the announcement of the death of Creighton, when the noble Crane, on whom all hearts were centred in the fearful peril of that hour, fell at the feet of his devoted comrades, pierced through the forehead by a rifle bullet. He spoke not a word—his strong heart ceased to beat; and his soul took its flight from its blood-red tenement, and from the confusion of battle, to the land of patriot spirits. He fell so far in the advance, that his men were driven back before possessing themselves of his body,—but soon after it was recovered.

The sketches of Creighton and Crane now lie in the same path.

After the bodies of the fallen braves had been laid side by side, the remaining few of a once full regiment gathered around and mourned,—the silence alone being broken by the tears and sobs of a band of warriors, grieving for the loss of their chieftains. Was such a scene ever witnessed? Those forms, now cold and bloody, had often led them on the field of carnage, to victory and glory; under their leadership the regiment had been made immortal; and now, in all their pride, and glory, and chivalry, they had gone down to rise no more. No wonder, then, that their brave followers paid their last tribute to all that was mortal of their renowned leaders. It seemed to these mourners, in their loss the regiment itself was blotted out—that it would no more be known and honored—that its sun had forever set. But no, many a brave heart, that stood in that circle, was to be made a sacrifice to his country; many more hearts were to be left crushed and bleeding for the loved ones fallen in battle. When the last tear had been shed, and the last vow made over these fallen braves, the regiment moved away in profound silence.

While this scene was being enacted afar off among the hills of Georgia, the peaceful valleys of Ohio were echoing with the lamentations of friends at home. The hearts of the people of the Western Reserve were bound by the strong ties of kin and friendship to this gallant regiment, which had but just made its great sacrifice, and they were all in mourning. When the news came of this great disaster, it could not be believed; the friends of the fallen would not give them up. And it was not until a dispatch was received that their bodies were on the way home, that it was generally believed. At last, when the people realized that the sad news was indeed true, meetings were called by the representatives of all branches of trade and industry. Resolutions of respect were passed, and preparations made to receive the dead, on their arrival, in a becoming manner.

When General Hooker learned of the death of Creighton and Crane, he raised both hands, in surprise and grief, exclaiming, "My God! are they dead? Two braver men never lived!"

General Butterfield, chief of staff, gave orders to remove the bodies to the rear. They were conveyed to Chattanooga by Sergeant Tisdell, where they were met by Quartermaster Loomis, and privates Wetzel, Shepherd, and Meigs. General Slocum testified his appreciation of their worth, by accompanying their bodies as far as Tullahoma. When the news reached him of their death, his grief was so profound, that the stern veteran burst into tears.

They were taken to Nashville to be embalmed. But little, however, could be done for Creighton, as he had bled inwardly; his body was therefore put into a metallic case. Crane's body was embalmed, and placed in a plain, but neat coffin, till it should arrive in Cleveland and be transferred to a burial case. Dr. Newbury, of the Sanitary Commission, rendered much service in this work, after which he accompanied the remains to Louisville. From this place they were forwarded to Cincinnati by train, where they were met by the special escort from Cleveland, consisting of Colonel Hayward, Lieutenant-Colonel J. T. Sterling, Lieutenant-Colonel Frazee, Captain Baird, Captain Molyneaux, Captain De Forest, Captain Wiseman, Surgeon Cushing, and Quartermaster Chapin.

On Sunday morning the train dashed into Cleveland, and stopped at the foot of Superior-street. Two hearses were in waiting. One for Colonel Creighton, drawn by four white horses; the other for Lieutenant-Colonel Crane, drawn by four black horses. Each was draped by American flags and the usual insignia of mourning.

The remains of Colonel Creighton were now removed from the car to the hearse, and conveyed to the residence of Mrs. Creighton, on Bolivar-street. The remains of Lieutenant-Colonel Crane remained under guard, till the return of the escort, when they were taken to the residence of the widow.

This bright Sabbath will long be remembered. But a few short Sabbaths before, the coffined dead left the city of their homes, possessed of life and hope: looking forward with pride and happiness to the termination of an honorable career in the service of their country. And often in their night vigils, over the dying embers of their picket-fires, had they conversed on the subject, passing the long night in dreams never to be realized. The remaining few of your followers have, indeed, long since returned; and although the hearts and feet of these brave warriors were heavy with the tramp of weary months, yet your slumber was not disturbed. Long years shall roll away, in which war's tumult and carnage shall cease; but you shall only be known among men by your good deeds left behind, and perpetuated in the hearts of your countrymen.

On the 7th of December the bodies of Creighton and Crane were brought from the residences of their families and taken to the Council Hall, for the purpose of lying in state, to be seen by the public. The same hearses were used as on the arrival of the bodies from the South.

The Council Hall was elegantly and appropriately decorated. In the centre, within the railing, a handsome canopy had been placed, with roof of national flags, draped with mourning emblems, suspended from the ceiling, and trailing at the corners to the ground. Wreaths, loops, and festoons of black and white edged the canopy. On the inside, from the centre, hung a large pendant of mourning emblems, beneath which was the bier on which lay the bodies of the gallant dead.

On the president's desk, at the head of the hall, were portraits of Colonel Creighton and Lieutenant-Colonel Crane, draped in mourning; and against the wall, behind the place of the president's seat, was a life-size portrait of Colonel Creighton, also draped in mourning. Above this portrait was this inscription, in black letters on white ground:

"My God! are they dead?

Two braver men never lived!"

—General Hooker.

The windows were hung with black, and the gaslights threw a dim, solemn light over the mournful scene.

The bodies were placed in handsome burial-cases, and the covers removed, so that they could be seen through the glass fronts. As we have before mentioned, the body of Colonel Creighton, from the wounds having bled inwardly, was so much changed, previously to reaching Nashville, that it was impossible to properly embalm it; and therefore did not present a natural appearance. That of Lieutenant-Colonel Crane was in good preservation, and could easily be recognized.

The bodies were guarded by a detachment of members of the old Seventh, who formed the guard of honor.

The following account of the funeral services is from the Cleveland Herald of the 9th of December.

"The sad pageant is over. A sorrowing people have paid their tribute of affection and regret over the remains of the dead heroes. The brave leaders of the glorious but ill-fated Seventh sleep in their quiet tomb.

"Tuesday, the 8th, was a bright and beautiful day. Its clear sky and pleasant atmosphere were strangely similar to that bright Sunday in May, two years and a half ago, when the Seventh Regiment marched out of Cleveland on its way to the battle-fields where it was destined to win such renown. The unclouded sun shed a halo of glory on all that was left of the brave men who led the old Seventh in many a fight; but who now were to be laid away in the silent and peaceful tomb.

"The bright day opened on a city of mourners. People gathered on the streets, waiting for the hour for the funeral. Business was unthought of, even the latest news by telegraph, exciting as it was, and calculated to stir the pulse with triumphant joy, failed to engross the attention. Men spoke of the dead heroes, of their first departure for the war, of their terrible battles and bloody sacrifices; and of that last fearful struggle on the hill at Ringgold, where the gallant leaders laid down their lives for their country, amid their dead and wounded comrades.

"From every flag-staff the national colors hung at half-mast, and signs of mourning were everywhere visible. As the hour set for the commencement of the solemn exercises drew near, business was entirely suspended throughout the city. The stores were closed, the Federal, State, and city offices shut their doors, and a Sabbath-like stillness reigned over the city. Soon came the tramp of armed men, the mournful wail of bugles, and the funeral roll of the drums, as the troops moved up to take part in the funeral procession.

"The bodies had remained in the Council Hall over-night, guarded by the old comrades of the gallant dead. The families and relatives were in the mayor's office, waiting for the hour of moving the procession. At half past ten o'clock the bodies were removed from the Council Hall and placed in hearses which were draped with the national colors, looped up with mourning emblems.

"The pall-bearers were as follows: For Colonel Creighton—Colonel Senter, Colonel Whittlesey, Major Mygatt, Lieutenant-Colonel Asper, Major Seymour, Captain McIlrath, Captain Ransom, Captain Stratton. For Lieutenant-Colonel Crane—Lieutenant-Colonel Goddard, Lieutenant-Colonel Sterling, Major Palmer, Captain Drummond, Captain Douglass, Captain Wilson, Captain Standart, Captain Hill.

"The burial-cases were the best that money could buy. On one was the following inscription:
Col. W. R. Creighton,
7th O. V. I,
In his 27th year.
Killed at the Battle of Ringgold,
Nov. 27th, 1863.

"On the other was the inscription:
Lieut.-Col. O. J. Crane,
Fell at the Battle of Ringgold,
Nov. 27th, 1863.

"On each coffin was laid a handsome wreath of immortelles, with the sword of the dead officer.

"The Twenty-ninth Volunteer Militia were drawn up in line each side of the way between the Council Hall and the Stone Church, and the mournful *cortege* passed through the lane so formed, Leland's Band playing a dirge. The hearse was followed by the mourners in carriages—Governor Brough, Surgeon McClurg, of the United States Military Hospital, the City Council, and City and County Officers, all wearing crape badges.

"Thousands of people lined the way, and crowded around the church with the hope of getting in; but there was not a sound from them, as the procession passed on to the church. And such perfect order and decorum we never before saw in such a vast concourse.

IN THE CHURCH.

"At the church—as indeed throughout the whole of the obsequies—the most perfect arrangements had been made, and were carried out. The reading-desk was draped with flags and crape. Directly in front was a stand with an elegant bouquet of flowers, and below this another stand, draped with national colors, on which rested the two coffins, side by side.

"The silk banner of the Seventh, presented by the city after Cross Lanes, and bearing the names of several battles, was displayed against the reading-desk. It was pierced and rent by showers of bullets and shell in many a hard-fought battle.

"The families and relatives of the deceased were placed in the seats immediately in front of the bodies. On either side of the coffins sat the pallbearers. Directly behind the mourners sat about a dozen or more of the members of the old Cleveland Light Guard, the company commanded by Colonel Creighton before the war, and of which Lieutenant-Colonel Crane was a member. They wore crape badges, and had with them the company flag, draped in mourning.

"Near the reading-desk were seated Governor Brough, Surgeon McClurg, and other invited guests, the committees, city council, city officers, county officers, the clergy of the city and neighborhood, members of the old Seventh, members of the old Cleveland Light Guard, soldiers from the Military Hospital, members of the Typographical Union, ship-carpenters, and other friends of the deceased. The body of the church was packed tightly with citizens, of whom the greater part were ladies, preference being given to them in the selection of seats. The Twenty-ninth Regiment stood in the aisles.

"During the entry of the procession to the church, the organ played a voluntary suitable to the occasion. At half-past eleven o'clock the funeral ceremonies in the church commenced with an invocation of the Divine blessing by Rev. S. W. Adams, of the First Baptist Church, who afterwards read appropriate passages of Scripture.

"The choir then sang the Ninetieth Psalm:
"'O God! our help in ages past,
Our help in years to come;
Our shelter from the stormy blast,
And our eternal home;
"'Beneath the shadow of Thy throne,
Thy saints have dwelt secure;
Sufficient is Thine arm alone,
And our defence is sure.

"'Before the hills in order stood,
Or earth received her name,
From everlasting Thou art God—
To endless years the same.
"'Thy word commands our flesh to dust:
Return ye sons of men!
All nations rose from earth at first,
And turn to earth again.
"'O God! our help in ages past,
Our help for years to come:
Be Thou our guide while troubles last,
And our eternal home.'

"Rev. Adam Crooks, of the Wesleyan Methodist Church, then made the following address, at the request of the family of the late Colonel Creighton:

"'To-day we are in the solemn presence of inexorable death. We are impressedly reminded that dust we are, and unto dust we must return; that "death is the mighty leveller of us all;" that "the tall, the wise, the heroic dead must lie as low as ours." Two lifeless heroes are before us—

"'Their swords in rust;
Their souls with God in heaven, we trust.'

We would do well to pray with the hero of other days: "So teach us to number our days, that we may apply our hearts unto wisdom." Before us are two more rich offerings which the State of Ohio and Cleveland have laid upon our country's altar! They were preceded by Wheeler, Lantry, Pickands, Mahan, Vail, and others. We are here to mourn, to honor, and to bury the noble dead! They were the pride of our city and of Northern Ohio. Brave and honored representatives of a brave and honored constituency! Of one thousand eight hundred soldiers who have filled the ranks of the Seventh Regiment Ohio Volunteer Infantry, but little over a hundred now report for duty. Many of them sleep in patriots' and heroes' graves. Most of the remainder bear on their persons honorable marks of their patriotism and bravery. In honoring the representative, we honor the constituency.

"'But *general* remarks are not appropriate from me. At the request of the stricken widow and relatives of Colonel Creighton, I come to utter a few words of condolence, sympathy, and comfort, in this hour, to *them* and *to us all*, of deep affliction. Brother Foot will speak in behalf of the relatives of Lieutenant-Colonel Crane.

"'Colonel William R. Creighton was born in the City of Pittsburgh, in the year 1836 or 1837—the records are not in this city. In early childhood he was bereft of a father. He was baptized by the Rev. Bishop Uphold, now bishop of Indiana, of the Protestant Episcopal Church.

"'In his early teens, he served in the employ of Mr. A———, in an extensive shoe establishment. Subsequently, he chose the occupation of a printer, and spent three years in making himself master of his trade. Eight years ago he came to this city —was four years in the office of the Cleveland Herald. Also some six months in the City of Chicago. At the time of enlistment, he was in the employ of Mr. Nevans of this city. Early in life, he gave evidence that the tendencies of his nature were strongly *military*.

"'This was evinced by his connection with companies for drill in Pittsburgh, Chicago, and this city. When the bloody drama of this dreadful war was inaugurated, he was lieutenant of the 'Cleveland Light Guard.' He was not willing that the fair and majestic superstructure, reared by the superior skill, patient labor, and heroic suffering of our honored fathers—resting its deep foundations in the inalienability of the natural rights of all men, and in which the most indigent son of toil stands before the law the equal peer of merchant princes—should be torn down by perjured traitors and sworn enemies of mankind; not willing that these traitors and enemies should bury beneath the magnificent ruins of this superstructure our strength, and greatness, and safety, and peace, and very liberties; not willing that this young, yet powerful republic, should be so dismembered and disintegrated as to tempt the rapacity, and be an easy prey of the weakest of adverse powers; not willing that the principle, that '*Capital shall own labor*,' the non-capitalled be the chattel of the rich, should rule all over this continent—that labor should be at once unremunerative and the badge of infamy, that thus there should be eternal antagonism between the indigent and the affluent, developing in intestine broils and civil feuds,—nor that the sun of liberty should go down upon an entire hemisphere, to rise not again for many generations; not willing that the forum, pulpit, and press should all be enslaved, and intelligence among the masses be rendered contraband; in brief, not willing that our *Paradise* should be converted into a *Pandemonium*.

"'Hence, no sooner had the news reached us of the assault upon Fort Sumter, and the call of the President for seventy-five thousand volunteers to rush to the defence of the life of the republic, than, with all the ardor of his earnest nature, Colonel William R. Creighton threw his *all* upon his country's altar, and appealed to his associates and compeers to do likewise.

"'His success in securing enlistments was commensurate with his zeal and known military skill. In a few days he was captain of a full company—the first enlisted in this city—which afterwards became Company A of the immortal Seventh Regiment Ohio Volunteer Infantry. On the morning of the 3d of May, 1861, a beautiful Sabbath morning in the spring, emblem of life, youth, and beauty, this regiment started for the field of conflict, glory, and of death. And now, on a clear, serene Sabbath of the December of 1863, the dying month of the year, the first Sabbath of the month, and in the morning, after many hard-fought battles, the brave colonel and lieutenant-colonel of the gallant Seventh came back to say to us, in the mute silence of death, 'We have done what we could.' In terms and strains of true eloquence you will soon be told by Brother Peck, how bravely the colonel led the charges at Cross Lanes, Winchester, Port Republic, Cedar Mountain (not at Antietam, for he was at home wounded), Dumfries, Chancellorsville, Gettysburg, Lookout Mountain, and fatal Ringgold,— and how he loved his brave command, and how they idolized him. But I will not anticipate, nor need I attempt encomium. His *deeds* praise him beyond the capacity of all human eloquence.

"'Of his *social* and *manly* qualities, one who knew him well is permitted to speak, in a letter of Christian sympathy, addressed to his widow—for the 2d of May, 1861, three days before leaving with his command, he was united in wedlock with Eleanor L. Quirk, of this city. In a letter, such as described above, the Rev. Mr. Brown, former pastor of Westminster Church, and for some months chaplain of the Seventh Regiment, says:

"'Mrs. Colonel Creighton: My dear Friend—I have just read in the dispatches that your brave husband and Lieutenant-Colonel Crane were killed in the late battle at Ringgold, Georgia. Oh, how sad this is! Sad to me who loved him; but how *terribly* sad to you, his beloved wife! I cannot write about it. Precious memories of hours and days of dangers and hardships, shared together in Western Virginia (and of one long, serious conversation about death and eternity, as we rode together at midnight through the woods) crowd upon me. He was warm-hearted, generous, and noble. He loved his country unto death. He was brave, even to rashness. But he has gone!'

"'Yes, the warm-hearted friend, the loving brother, the affectionate son, the devoted husband, the brave soldier, the undying patriot, the fearless and fiery Creighton, is gone! We are here to-day to honor his memory, recount his heroic deeds of noble daring, mourn his fall, and convey his lifeless remains—with those of his brave comrade, Lieutenant-Colonel Crane—to the tomb of a hero and a patriot.

"'What words of elegiac comfort shall I speak to his numerous personal and sorrowful friends; his brothers in the union of the same useful and honorable handicraft; his brave comrades in arms of the noble Seventh, and other regiments, who are here to attest their affection and sorrow; his brother in the flesh, who is now left without a brother; his aged and sorely bereaved mother; and his youthful, but grief-stricken, widow? How shall *I*, who would take my place with the mourners, speak words of comfort to you?

"'Let us remember that although our *dear, dear* friend will no longer mingle with us in the social or domestic circle,—will not again lead regiment or brigade of fearless braves in the thickest and hottest of the fight, inspiring to feats of exalted heroism—his brave and generous heart now cold and lifeless—dim and sightless those eyes whose radiant and enlivening orbs beamed, now with kindness, and now with fiery bravery—his intercourse with the living world, brought to a final period,—let us remember, that although Colonel Creighton is gone, yet he is not lost; he is not lost to his country, for it has his noble example of true bravery and practical patriotism.

"'He is not lost to us who knew him, for he lives, and will ever live, templed in our brightest memories and best affections. Nor can he be lost to history, for he has made the offering which places his name on its brightest page.

"'Death never comes alone, but is always attended by an escort of sadness. Whenever the silver cord is loosed, the golden bowl broken, the pitcher broken at the fountain, the wheel broken at the cistern, and dust returns to the earth, as it was, mourners go about the streets. But it is especially sad, when, as in this case, sister, mother, and wife are denied the sorrowful pleasure of being present, and ministering to the wants of the dying, and speaking words of Christian hope. But even this finds an offset in the fact that it was his honored privilege to die for country—to fall, covered with glory! Also, in the fact that his body was not mangled—that he did not suffer long—in the assurance furnished by the words, 'Oh, my dear wife!' uttered in dying accents after he fell, and before he expired, that his last thoughts were of home and kindred; and may not we hope that these words were breathed in prayer, and that he threw his whole soul helpless, but trustfully, upon the merits of the Saviour? Again, it is a source of great gratification to us all, and especially to the relatives, that he does not fill a distant and unknown grave—that he was tenderly borne from the field, and promptly forwarded for honorable interment. His grave is to be in our midst, marked by a marble shaft, which will scarcely crumble beneath the tread of the coming ages. You can go there and pay the mournful tribute which nature and affection prompt. And may it not be believed, that from their patriotic ashes (for Creighton and Crane fought and fell together, and they are to rest side by side)—is it not to be believed, that from their patriotic ashes will spring a rich harvest *in kind* to at once avenge their fall, and save our imperilled country? And will not fathers and mothers conduct their children to these honored graves, and there put upon them vows of eternal hostility to treason and to traitors, be they secret or armed, even as Hamilcar caused his son Hannibal to swear, at the altar, eternal hatred to Rome? And will not every one who visits their tombs, and reads their epitaphs, whisper, "Peace and honor." And when this cruel war is over, and the God of our fathers shall crown our labors and sufferings with success, and bestow upon us, as a nation, an honorable, righteous, and perpetual peace, then, amid the light, and songs, and joy of the nation's jubilee, let their epitaphs be written anew. And during all ages, peace to their ashes, peace to their memory, and peace to their heroic spirits.

"'Let us this day, around the lifeless forms of these fallen heroes, not profanely, but solemnly and religiously, swear that the lives of these, together with the lives of hundreds of thousands of the flower of the nation, given for the salvation of the country, shall not be given in vain; that we will complete well, what they have so well begun.

"'I need not ask of you, in behalf of the aged mother and bereaved widow of Colonel Creighton, your warm, your practical, your continued sympathies: these, I am sure, will not be withheld. But I now ask you to join me in one fervent prayer to the God of the aged, the fatherless, and the widow, our fathers' God, and the God of battles, that He will, by His almighty arm, sustain, and, by His abundant grace, comfort the aged mothers, and bereaved widows, and afflicted friends of our brave soldiers, and their departed sons, husbands, and brothers; that He will thus sustain and comfort all whose hearts have been cloven by the battle-axe of war; that He will abundantly shield, help, bless, and comfort our brave soldiers upon the field, in the hospitals, and prisoners in the hands of our enemies; and that He will speedily bestow upon our imperilled country the inestimable blessing of an honorable, righteous, and lasting peace. Amen.'

"Rev. C. C. Foot, at the request of the family of the late Lieutenant-Colonel Crane, made the following address:

"'The duties we are called to perform—the bearing of our dead brave to their final rest—is indeed solemn and sad. That those who admired and loved them in life, and delight to honor them when dead, should, with sympathizing hearts and grateful hands, minister such a funeral ovation, is due to them in view of the sacrifice they made, the toils they endured, and their deeds of patriotism and valor. When the bugle was first sounded in Washington, calling the North to the defence of our institutions, these were among the first to respond; leaving their business, their friends, and their families, for the field of strife, they unsheathed their swords to strike for freedom's sacred cause. In many skirmishes, and in every battle of their brigade, they struck with such bravery and success as to have secured perpetual illustriousness; while ever a nation exists to feel the throb of a nation's heart, while a man lives to read the annals of America, their noble deeds shall be known, and their illustrious names shall be honored.

"'They passed through so many dangers almost unscarred, that they feared no ill, and their families began to expect with confidence their return to the enjoyments of home, ere many months more should have flown. But when on Ringgold's hillside they raised their swords to gleam as never before, from a volley of Confederate musketry their death-warrant came. Their bodies sank to the ground—their spirits ascended through the smoke-cloud of battle to the patriot's God, to join the slain of the Seventh Ohio Volunteer Infantry, where the stars forever shine in original splendor and glory. On the morrow, instead of the ready pen reporting to loved ones at home that "all is well with us," the telegraph was put in requisition to announce that never more should their voices be heard by friend, companion, or offspring. Oh, how sad such intelligence! How many families, how many tender, loving, trembling hearts throughout the land, have been made sorrowful by like intelligence since this war was so cruelly hurled upon us? From what our soldier friends do and suffer from the myriad untimely deaths, shall we not learn the magnitude of the work of the army, and our great indebtedness to all who have gone to fight for us, our homes, and our country? Let us render them the honor due. When men become illustrious, it is but natural that their friends review their lives, and that others inquire who they are, whence they came, and what circumstances molded them for their greatness. To answer briefly and in part such inquiries about one of these brave men—Lieutenant-Colonel O. J. Crane—is the work to which I have been invited. Lieutenant-Colonel Crane was born in Chautauque County, New York, in the year 1829. When about three years old, his parents removed to their native State, Vermont. Soon after this, his father died, and he was left to climb life's rugged hill from his mother's arms to manhood, without the invaluable aid of a father's counsels and assistance. He was blest with a kind, intelligent, and prayerful mother, to whom he owed no small amount of gratitude.

"'Her care and labor for his health, and even his life, were constant and great. While quite young, he once received a burn, so severe that his life was despaired of. The attendant physician said he could not live—or living, would always be helpless. But his mother loved him into *life* and *health*, little thinking that she had saved him from one fire, only to see him exposed and becoming a victim to a more galling one; little thinking that to him, for whose life she struggled, she and the nation would become indebted for liberty and political security. During his youth he lived chiefly with an uncle, and with whom, about thirteen years ago, he located in Conneaut, Ohio. While there, he was employed in mechanical labor. He spent one year on the Isthmus. On his return from the Isthmus, he came to Cleveland, and found employment as a ship-carpenter. In this city, and this business, he remained till called to participate in our national conflict.

"'As a mechanic, he enjoyed the confidence and esteem of his employers and his fellows. As a man, he drew around him a pleasant circle of friends, constant and affectionate, who deeply mourn his loss. In disposition, he was frank, manly, kind, and ever cheerful. He leaves a sorrowing wife, to whom he was married nine years ago, three small children, a mother, brothers and sisters. Their bereavement is too great, their grief too deep, for even them to express in language. Yet not till weary weeks shall fail to bring letters from the battle-field—not till months confirm that no husband returns—not till years reveal the need of a father to guide the orphans, and a companion to sustain an aching heart, shall be fully realized the magnitude of the sacrifice made, in laying upon a nation's altar a husband and a father.

"'The subject of these remarks had never made a public profession of faith in Jesus. He had respected religion. He showed great kindness and respect to the chaplain of his regiment, and consequently had a good chaplain. He also, after entering the service, became interested in personal religion. He professed a readiness to die when called. Let us pray and hope that beyond the turmoil of this life, he may receive his dear ones to everlasting fellowship of joy.

"'Some months ago he became a member of the Masonic fraternity. Though so soon taken from them, yet—

"'By the hieroglyphic bright,
Which none but craftsmen ever saw,
Strange memory on our minds shall write
His honored name that's far awa.'

"'Citizens of Cleveland and Ohio, as we embalm his name in our memory, let us not fail to remember, also, the dear family he has left. Let us give them our heartfelt sympathy—not the sympathy of *pity*, but that of *gratitude*—for his and their debtors we are. He gave his life; not for himself, but for us who live, for our homes, and our posterity. Surrounding the husbandless with what comforts we can, and supplying the fatherless with fatherly care, and aid, and sympathy, let us, to our utmost, discharge our indebtedness. Let us work and pray that but few more brave need fall; and that the time be speeded when the defenders of our liberties shall be welcomed home to the enjoyment of their triumphs, with the jubilant acclamation of many millions of freemen.'

"Professor H. E. Peck, at the request of the General Committee, delivered the address on behalf of the city, as follows:

"'On a fair Sabbath in May, only three short seasons ago, just as the bells were calling the town to worship, a regiment passed down yonder street. That, citizens, was a spectacle which you who saw it will never forget. Not because the marching column was striking to the eye. There was no pageant. There were no arms, no banners. There was not even a uniform. The farmer, the student, and the smith, were in that line; and the farmer marched in the garments he brought from the furrow, and the student and the smith were attired as they had been in the recitation-room and shop. But for all that, the display was profoundly impressive. Here was the flower of the Reserve. Lake, Mahoning, Trumbull, Lorain, and Erie, each had a hundred; Portage, twice a hundred; and Cuyahoga, thrice a hundred in the line. And each hundred was made up, not of the rabble, but of sons, whom worthy fathers and mothers dearly loved; of men, who, if they should stay at home, would soon be conspicuous for wealth, or learning, or skill in useful arts. And these thousand true men, loved well at home, made of sterling stuff, were on their way to *war*—to actual war. To serve the imperilled country, they had quit all, —farms, shops, books, friends, hopes, the past, the future,—all but duty and honor. They might never return. The vow on them might take them to bloody fields, from which there should be no passage except down through the gates of death. Oh, kinsman, was not that an impressive scene? Did you ever see the like? Did not tears wet your eyes as you looked on? Were not the cheers with which you sent the heroes on their way divided, as shouts of yours had never before been, nor have been since, between admiration and sorrow?

"'This, friends, was the first march of our gallant Seventh. You do not forget that in that march the column was led by a young captain, whose high carriage and soldierly bearing were almost the only signs of real military display. The body of that young captain lies in one of yonder coffins. Of him, and his brave comrade who sleeps beside him, I am to speak on this occasion. The history of the noble Seventh is *their* late history. With it, therefore, let me begin.

"'The Seventh left Cleveland May 5, 1861. It went hence to Camp Dennison, where E. B. Tyler, of Ravenna; W. R. Creighton, of Cleveland; and John S. Casement, of Painesville, were made its first field-officers. In the June following, while it was still at Camp Dennison, the regiment was reorganized and sworn into the three-years' service. I well remember seeing Captain Crane, whose remains are yonder, on a sweet Sabbath afternoon—men, sun, air, and earth, all were glad, and the harmonies of nature were tunefully praising God—bringing his company to the colonel's quarters to be sworn in. I well remember the impression which the strong voice of the sombre captain made upon me, as, after the young soldiers, with bare heads and uplifted hands, had taken the oath, he cried, "Company, right face; forward, march!" The tone of the command was as if he would say, "Now, men, there is no retreat. Only service, perhaps death, is before you."

"'A week later, General McClellan, who had then just taken command of the Western Department, came looking for the right material with which to begin his Western Virginia campaign, and inspected the regiment. But it was not at garments the shrewd leader looked. It was the *person* he studied. He sought the eye. He narrowly scanned the look. Down the line and back again he slowly went. I saw the expression on his face, as at the end, he seemed to say to himself, "*They are the right sort!*" In the reorganization of the regiment, the staff remained as it was before.

"'On the 26th of June, 1861, the Seventh left Camp Dennison, to enter on active service in Western Virginia. With many long marches it sought the foe. It had begun to doubt whether it would ever meet him, when, at Cross Lanes, on the 26th of August, he came, with overwhelming force. For a brief space, the companies, separated from each other, held their ground. Then, from bare and irresistible necessity, they gave way. Twenty-four gallant men were left on the field, dead or wounded. One hundred were carried away prisoners, and the remainder were scattered like partridges which have received the sportsman's fire. At first, tidings came to us that the Seventh was wholly destroyed. How ached our hearts! Presently, better news came. Major Casement had brought four hundred men through the wilderness into Charleston, and Captain Crane had come to Gauley, bringing, not only almost his entire company, but a flag which he had captured from the enemy.

"'Then came to the regiment days of distraction and despondency. You, and others of the Reserve, heard of, and agonized over its condition. To encourage and cheer it, you sent it a stand of beautiful colors. At the Academy of Music, as you will remember, before a throng of your best citizens, the standards were dedicated.

"'On a mountain-side, in Western Virginia, with Rosecrans' army lying miles up and down, and with the smoke of the enemy's camp-fires rising in the distance, they were presented to the regiment. I wish I could picture the scene, the splendors of the magnificent landscape, the exquisite beauty of the colors as they proudly glowed in the clear sunlight, the enthusiasm of the men and the pride of the officers. Your present helped to rouse the spirit of the regiment. The words of love and considerate regard, which you sent with the gift, assured it that its honor was not yet lost. How thrilling, how hopeful, was the cheer which rolled off among the hills, as the color-guard took its trust!

"'From the Kanawha the Seventh went, on the 17th of December, 1861, to the Potomac. There, now led by Lieutenant Colonel Creighton—Colonel Tyler having taken temporary command of a brigade—it met, at Winchester, March 23, 1862, Jackson's celebrated "Stonewall Legion." Hot was the fire, when the Northern iron met the Southern flint. The Seventh left fifty-six dead and wounded on the field. But it won a name in the fight. The story told of them, the land over, was, *they fought like veterans*. Then came the long chase up the Shenandoah, then the hard march across to Eastern Virginia, and back to the gates of the Shenandoah. Then came Port Republic, the first square stand-up fight which the regiment had, when, led by Creighton, in an open field, in a line trim enough for a dress parade, and with "Cross Lanes" for its battle-cry, the glorious Seventh charged down on Jackson's steadfast front. Ah, how the list of the dead and wounded was again fearfully swelled! Seventy-two names were added to it.

"'By this time the regiment had become so reduced by the casualties of war, that its friends on the Reserve asked that it might be sent home to recruit. "No," promptly replied discriminating Halleck, "not so long as there is a lame drummer left; not if you will send us a whole new regiment in place of this handful. We know these men, they are just such as we want." Colonel Tyler's promotion to a brigadiership brought Lieutenant-Colonel Creighton to the head of the regiment, and this, and other changes, presently made Captain Crane a Lieutenant-Colonel. The regiment now had plenty of duty. It fought at Cedar Mountain, and there, on the extreme advance, it met the brunt of danger.

"'In one company, out of twenty-one men engaged, eighteen fell killed or wounded. The whole regiment suffered in hardly less proportion. One hundred and ninety-six, of the two hundred and ninety-seven heroes engaged, fell. There, fiery Creighton, as usual, not content to be elsewhere than on the extreme front, was so severely wounded that he was compelled to come home to recover.

"'Soon the regiment was at Antietam, and there it shared the toils and honors of that honorable field. Thirty-eight fallen men, out of one hundred engaged, was the price it paid for its opportunity. Presently it fought and prevailed against great odds at Dumfries. Here it lost ten more of its scant few.

"'In the next year's campaign, after lying in camp and being considerably recruited, the regiment was at Chancellorsville. There it did good service, by catching and holding on its steady line droves of fugitives, who were ingloriously seeking the rear, and by covering the retreat of its corps. It lost, at Chancellorsville, ninety-nine men. Next the regiment was at Gettysburg. There, for the first time in its history, it fought behind defences; nor could Ewell, surging with fiery valor up against the rocky rampart, break the line which it, and its compeers of the Twelfth Corps, held. The Seventh lost at Gettysburg nineteen men; and, as from every field before, so from this, it brought honor and a new name. From the Potomac the regiment went, in September last, to the Tennessee. There, on the 24th of last month, it shared in that brilliant "battle above the clouds," by which Hooker cleared Lookout Mountain. Decisive as the result of its courage here was, it seems to have left behind but one wounded man as its share of the sacrifice which the victory cost. Then came the pursuit of Bragg, and the overtaking of his rear-guard at Ringgold; then the climbing, by the Twelfth Corps, of that bare hill, on the top of which the enemy was securely posted. Staunch Creighton was in command of a brigade, and Crane led the Seventh. The charge was a desperate one, but Creighton did not falter. Kindling to that ardor of which he was so susceptible, he urged his command on. "Boys," he said, "we are ordered to take that hill. I want to see you walk right up it." Then putting himself, not in the rear, as being temporarily a brigadier he might have done, but far in the advance, he led the way. And Crane, close behind, stoutly held the Seventh to its bloody work. The men were ready for the task. The zeal of Cross Lanes, of Winchester, of Port Republic, burned to a white heat. The gallant Seventh, leading the column, flung itself into the billows of fire, as if it were rescuing home from robber hands. But, ah! chivalric Creighton fell, and, alas! sturdy Crane, too; and of the commissioned officers of the Seventh, but one remained unhurt. Is it wonderful that the grand old regiment, losing the inspiring command of the brave soldiers whose voices had so often aroused its purposes, fell back? Oh, Creighton and Crane, had you lived, the Seventh would, perhaps, without help, have carried the dear old colors, tattered by so many leaden storms, into the enemy's defiant works! Sad tale that I must tell, of the two hundred and ten sons and brothers of ours who went into the fight, ninety fell; of the fourteen commissioned officers on the field, thirteen were killed or wounded.

"'My story of the Seventh is done. Yes, the Sabbath comes; sweet, clear day, as bright as that holy morn on which the Seventh first went its way. A sad cortege passes up the same street yonder. Music wails at its head. A downcast guard of honor marches, with mourning colors, behind hearses trimmed with the badges of woe. Look you, kindred, the band which follows the dead is made up of the men who marched in that May Sabbath line two years ago. But the farmer, the student, the smith, are not there. These are soldiers all. They are scarred with the marks of Cross Lanes, of Winchester—nay, let me not stop to recite the long list of battles through which they have passed. Yes, here is part of the scant few left out of the eighteen hundred staunch men who have stood under the flag of the Seventh; and here, hearse-borne, are the bodies of the good leaders who shall head the regiment no more. Pause now, citizens, while I tell you about these noble men. Colonel Creighton was born in Pittsburgh. He was but twenty-six years of age when he fell. For several years he followed the trade of a printer in this city. But he was born to be a soldier, and years ago he learned, in civic schools, a soldier's trade. So, when the war broke out, he was fit to take command. He raised a company in this city. At once his military talent was revealed. He had not a peer in the camp as a drill-master, and there was something about his ardent nature which made men feel that he was fit to command. Thus superior office came to him—he did not seek it. But getting it, he discharged his duties well. He was affectionate to his men, erring only in being, perhaps, too free with them. And when battle came, he was a master-spirit in the dreadful storm. Burning with enthusiasm, almost rash with courage, he could inspire his "gamecocks"—as he familiarly called his men—with such qualities as are most needed in the charge and in the deadly breach. I have often asked sound thinking members of the Seventh, "What of Creighton?" The answer has always been, "*He is a soldier, every inch.*"

"'Lieutenant-Colonel Crane was born in Troy, New York, in the year 1828. He, too, has been a mechanic here for many years. Like his chief, he, too, had learned the use of arms before the war commenced. He was, therefore, amply qualified to take command of his company when Captain Creighton was promoted. And no ordinary disciplinarian was Captain Crane. He had a difficult company, but it was with a strong hand that he laid hold of his work. Headstrong men had a master in him. Withal, he was the soul of kindness to those he commanded. His rugged nature, despising military finery, and the pomps and forms of military life, came down at once to plain, blunt, frank, but sincere and hearty intercourse with the men under him. If you wished to find Captain Crane, you must look for him where his boys were; and if his boys had had a trying or toilsome work, you might be sure he was lightening the load by his own example of brave and sturdy patience. He did not have an impulsive nature. He was not a thunderbolt on the field. He was rock, rather. Fiery floods might break against him, and yet he was always the same; always imperturbable, honest, strong.

"'I should have said before, that Colonel Creighton was in every battle which the Seventh ever fought, except Antietam. It is in place for me to say here, that Lieutenant-Colonel Crane took part in every battle in which his regiment shared. I doubt if another instance of the kind is on record. Would that the Hand which had so often averted danger, could have turned the fatal bullets aside at Ringgold!

"'And now, friends, I am, at the invitation of the joint-committee of the city council, the military, the Typographical Union, the ship-carpenters, and yourselves, and as the representative of other towns, who helped raise the Seventh, to bring a tribute of gratitude and praise to the memory of the gallant dead. In my poor way, I here certify to the noble qualities, to the brave deeds of the soldiers coffined yonder. I come to say, that the honor done them by the city, by the military, by yourselves, by good men who, in other towns, mourn their loss, is well bestowed. The heroes have earned their honors. They have bought them with such high conduct, with such self-sacrifices, as the brightest laurels poorly reward. I know not how those souls, which lately inhabited yonder clay, stand in the other world (would that your prayers and mine could reach them), but I do know, that their names shall live in this world forever. The marble you shall put up over their dust will itself have gone to dust before their renown shall have passed from the hearts and lips of men.

"'Would, friends, that you and I, by any ministry of love, could staunch these widows' and half-orphans' tears. Oh! sisters bereaved, and dear little children, now fatherless, may God in His mercy keep you! May He be help and hope to you! Remember, I pray you, that the spilled blood which was so dear to you, was precious also to God; that it is from such seed that He makes freedom, peace, social order, and prosperity to grow.

"'And, citizens, what shall I say of the Seventh, which mourns its noble dead? Shall I summon here the spirits of those who have fallen on the half-score fields, where the staunch old regiment has left its dead? Shall I call from the shadowy world those who have died in festering prisons? Shall I order the rally for those who, broken in body, shall engage in active pursuits no more? Shall I bring from the field the little remnant—headed by the one unhurt commissioned officer, and under this dear, chafed, and rent old flag, which no longer shines with the glory of color and figure which it displayed when first unfurled in your Academy of Music, but which is lustrous with the light with which brave deeds have invested it

—shall I tell them of your love for, and your gratitude to them? Nay, this I cannot do. But I can say to these representatives of the regiment who are with us, and through them to that little handful of bronzed veterans who, huddling around a single camp-fire at Chattanooga, are the last remnant of the Seventh—to you, honored men, we owe a debt we can never discharge. You sprang to arms, when others hesitated. You entered the flinty paths of war with feet shod only for the gentle ways of peace. Often have you been tried, never have you failed; and the honor of the Reserve, which we committed to you, has been proudly kept on every field. And in this hour of weighty bereavement, our feelings towards you and your comrades, living and dead, is like that of the pious Scotch woman who, when grim Claverhouse having first shot her husband, laughing, asked, "Well, woman, what thinkest thou of thy good man now?" quietly replied, as she drew the pierced head to her bosom, and wiped the death-damp from his brow: "I aye thought much of him, but now more than ever."

"'Now, bearers, take out your dead. Put the cherished remains in an honored place. Tell art to lift above them worthy marble. Write upon the stone the names of the battles in which our heroes have fought. Write also the virtues of the dead. Write, too, that gratitude has lifted the monument, partly to do honor to them, worthy of it, whom human praise can never reach; and to teach the living that it is well to make even life a sacrifice to duty. And when our war has been ended, when peace and freedom shall be in all our borders, thronging feet shall, through all the generations, come up to your memorial, and learn lessons of heroism and self-sacrifice.'

"Rev. William Goodrich, of the First Presbyterian Church, made the closing prayer; after which the choir chanted impressively the following hymn:

"'With tearful eyes I look around,
Life seems a dark and gloomy sea;
Yet midst the gloom I hear a sound,
A heavenly whisper, 'Come to Me.'

"'It tells me of a place of rest—
It tells me where my soul may flee;
Oh! to the weary, faint, oppressed,
How sweet the bidding, 'Come to Me!'

"'When nature shudders, loth to part
From all I love, enjoy, and see,
When a faint chill steals o'er thy heart,
A sweet voice utters, 'Come to Me.'

"'Come, for all else must fade and die,
Earth is no resting place for thee;
Heavenward direct thy weeping eye,
I am thy portion, 'Come to Me.'

"'Oh, voice of mercy! voice of love!
In conflict, grief, and agony;
Support me, cheer me from above!

And gently whisper, Come to Me.'
"This closed the exercises at the church.
THE FUNERAL PROCESSION.

"As soon as the exercises in the church closed, the Brooklyn Light Artillery commenced firing minute-guns from the field-piece planted on the square in front of the church. At the same time, the chimes of Trinity rang a muffled peal, and the bells in all the other churches commenced tolling. The square and the streets leading to it were packed with people from the city and surrounding country, the latter having been pouring in all the morning. It seemed almost impossible to keep an open space in so great a crowd, but the admirable management of the marshals of the day and the city police, aided by the spirit of order and decorum in the crowd, succeeded in preventing any trouble or confusion.

"The procession was formed in nearly the order as at first arranged. First came Leland's band, playing the "Dead March." Then the Twenty-ninth Regiment, commanded by Lieutenant-Colonel Frazee, with arms reversed and bound with crape. Next the discharged officers and soldiers of the Seventh, headed by their old band. These old members of the regiment numbered sixty, and were formed into a company, under Captain Molyneaux. They were followed by the clergymen of the city, after which came the bodies.

"Colonel Creighton's body was in a hearse drawn by four white horses, from undertaker Duty; and the body of Lieutenant-Colonel Crane, in a hearse drawn by four black horses, from undertaker Howland. Behind the hearses were led two horses fully caparisoned. The pall-bearers, whose names have been previously given, walked beside the hearses. Eleven carriages, containing the mourners, came next, followed by a carriage containing Lieutenant Loomis, Sergeant-Major Tisdel, Bugler Welzel, and privates Shepherd and Meigs, forming the escort from the Seventh. Next were the members of the old Cleveland Light Guard, with their badges and flags; Governor Brough and other invited guests, committee of arrangements, city council, city officers, county military committee, two hundred sick and wounded soldiers from the United States Military Hospital, soldiers from the Twelfth Cavalry, Brooklyn Light Artillery, Captain Pelton; other military and officers of the United States regular and volunteer services; United States Court officers, Typographical Union, ship-carpenters, old Light Guard, under Captain J. Robinson, students from Commercial College, County Court officers, citizens on foot, citizens in carriages.

"The procession was of great length, and passed through a dense crowd of thousands of people during the whole way. It was well managed by Colonel William H. Hayward, chief marshal of the day, and his assistants, H. M. Chapin, William Edwards, John M. Sterling, junior, and C. Busch. The police were again of incalculable value in clearing the way and keeping perfect order.

AT THE TOMB.

"The lot in the Woodland Cemetery, intended as the final resting-place of the heroic dead, not having yet been selected, the bodies were taken to the City Cemetery, and deposited temporarily in the Bradburn Vault, the use of which had been generously tendered. The police again, ever vigilant and effective, had kept the cemetery and its approaches free from the vast crowd until the procession had entered, and then secured ample room, so that there was no crowding or confusion.

"The Twenty-ninth Regiment was drawn up in line, with colors immediately opposite the tomb. The company of the old members of the Seventh, with reversed arms, stood at the right of the tomb.

"As the procession moved up to the tomb the band played a dirge. The Rev. W. A. Fiske, rector of Grace Church, read the beautiful and impressive burial-service of the Episcopal Church, the bodies were placed in the vault, the final prayer said, and then the door of the tomb was closed. The old members of the Seventh fired three volleys over the tomb, and all was over. The heroic dead sleep undisturbed.

"So ended the grandest and the most mournful pageant that has passed through the streets of Cleveland for many a year."

LIEUT.-COL. MERVIN CLARK.

On a gloomy night in May, 1861, when the wind was howling in fitful gusts, and the rain pouring down in merciless rapidity, the writer was awakened by the stentorian voice of the adjutant in front of the tent, followed by an order that Lieutenant —— would report for guard-duty. After wading half-knee deep in mud and water, narrowly escaping a cold bath in an over-friendly ditch, I arrived at the headquarters of the guard. Soon after my arrival, a boy reported to me for duty, as sergeant of the guard; a position no less responsible than my own. At first I felt that, on such a fearful night, I needed more than a boy to assist me in the performance of my task. His form was fragile; his face was smooth as that of a girl, and in the dim, shadowy light of a camp-fire, struggling against the heavy rain, I took him to be about fifteen years of age. We immediately entered into conversation, and between admiration and surprise, the rain was forgotten, and the moments sped so rapidly, that it was nearing the time to change the guard. But my boy companion had forgotten nothing, and as the moment arrived, he called in the relief. As he moved among those sturdy warriors, it occurred to me that I had never before met a boy, who was at the same time a man—a brave, prudent, reliable man. All night he did his duty, and when we parted in the morning, I both loved and admired him. This was my first meeting with Colonel Clark.

Mervin Clark was a native of Ohio, having been born in the city of Cleveland, in 1843. When but three years of age his mother died, and at the age of nine his surviving parent, leaving him an orphan. He was now taken, into the family of Henry W. Clark, an uncle, where he found a home, and kind friends, during the remainder of his life.

The flash of the last gun at Sumter had hardly died away, when he enrolled himself as a private in Captain De Villiers' company, at the same time declaring that he would, by no act of his, leave the service of his country, until rebels in arms were met and subdued. How well he kept that pledge, it is the office of this brief sketch to show.

He left Camp Dennison as an orderly-sergeant, and during the trying marches and skirmishes in Western Virginia, won a commission. Arriving in the East, he was made a first-lieutenant. At the battle of Winchester, he surprised and delighted every one who saw him. When the bullets flew thickest, he stepped on to the brink of the hill, over which our men were firing, and, with revolver in hand, took part in the strife. His captain, seeing his danger, directed him to get behind a tree which stood close by. He obeyed orders, but with his back to the tree, and his face to the foe. At the battle of Cedar Mountain, he commanded a company, and during that fearful day, led his men with great bravery. At last, when the order was given to retreat, he mistook it for an order to charge, and, with a dozen men, dashed at the double line of a whole brigade of rebels. It was not until an officer of authority conveyed the true order to him, that he would withdraw. He now took part in all the battles in which his regiment was engaged in the East, except Antietam. When the regiment left for the West, he accompanied it, and soon after took part in the battles of Lookout Mountain, Mission Ridge, Taylor's Ridge, and the series of engagements taking place while with Sherman. Before his term of service expired, he was made a captain, and commanded his company on its homeward march. He was soon after mustered out with his company. He now sought quiet and rest at his home, giving no evidence of an intention to again enter the service. But before he had been at home many weeks, he surprised and disappointed his friends by enlisting as a private in the regular army. His fame, however, was too wide-spread in Ohio to suffer him to re-enter the service as a private. Governor Brough had already selected him for promotion, and when learning of his enlistment in the regular service, procured an order for his discharge, and immediately appointed him lieutenant-colonel of the One Hundred and Eighty-third Regiment, then about to enter the field. He had now come of age, November 5th, and on the 8th of November cast his first vote; on the 12th, he received his commission; and on the 15th, he left for the front. His regiment joined the army of General Thomas, on its retreat before the rebel forces under Hood. On the 30th of November, the regiment was engaged in the terrible battle of Franklin. During the engagement, the regiment was ordered to charge the enemy's works. The color bearer was soon shot down, when Clark seized the colors, and calling to his men, "Who will follow me to retake these works?" mounted the rebel works, and immediately fell, a minie ball having passed through his head. Every effort was made to take his body from the field, but to no purpose, and the "boy officer" was wrapped in his blanket, and buried on the field of his fame, to be finally removed by careful hands, when the earth had covered every vestige of the strife in its friendly bosom.

LIEUTENANT HENRY ROBINSON.

Henry Robinson was a native of Ohio, and entered the service as first-lieutenant of Company G. He was always attentive to his duties, and soon took a position among the first of his rank. He was constantly with his command during its early service. He was in the skirmish at Cross Lanes, where he won the respect and confidence of the entire command by his gallant conduct. In this affair, he commanded Company G. Arriving at Charleston, he was sent to Gauley Bridge, and soon after was taken violently sick with a fever. He soon after died.

In the death of Lieutenant Robinson, the regiment made one of its greatest sacrifices. He was esteemed by every one for his kind and courteous manners, as well as for his ability as a soldier. He had many friends in the army, and at home, and I doubt very much if he had an enemy in the world. His military career was short, but of such a character that his friends can refer to it with pride.

LIEUTENANT E. S. QUAY.

E. S. Quay entered the service as second-lieutenant of Company G. He was with the regiment at Cross Lanes, where he gave promise of much future usefulness as a soldier. He accompanied the regiment to Eastern Virginia, where he was acting assistant adjutant-general to Colonel Tyler. He took part in the battle of Winchester, where he did splendid service. After Tyler's promotion to a general, he was made adjutant-general, and assigned to his staff. In this capacity, he served in the battle of Port Republic, where he gained new laurels. He finally went to his home on account of ill-health, and after a time, died of consumption. He was a good soldier.

LIEUTENANT JAMES P. BRISBINE.

James P. Brisbine was a native of Trumbull County, Ohio. He was born in 1836. His parents dying while he was quite young, he went to live with an uncle by the name of Applegate. He received a fair education, and during the time, in part, maintaining himself by teaching school in winter. In the spring of 1860, he commenced reading law in Warren, Ohio, which he continued until the breaking out of the rebellion. During his course of study, he gave promise of an able and useful lawyer. When it became evident that the rebellion could not be suppressed but by the force of arms, he deemed it his duty to leave the study of the profession of his choice, and enroll himself among the defenders of his country. This step he considered as a decided sacrifice to him; for, by nature, he was in no way inclined to the life of a soldier; he preferred the quiet life of a citizen, which is alone to be found at home. It was with many misgivings that he finally placed his name on the roll. In doing this, he was alone influenced by patriotic motives. When urged to be a candidate for the position of sergeant, he declined to have any thing to do with the matter; but was elected, notwithstanding his indifference.

At Camp Dennison, he was made orderly-sergeant. He took part in the skirmish at Cross Lanes, where he made a good record as a soldier. Soon after entering the field, his health failed him. The long marches often taxed him beyond his strength; but he seldom complained. He was not in the battle of Winchester on account of sickness, being disabled from the effects of the severe march from Strasburg, which took place a short time before. He expressed many regrets on account of his absence. But he very soon had an opportunity to test his courage on the battle-field. The engagement of Port Republic occurred shortly after. He was in no respect second in gallantry to those who were in the previous battle. He was ever at his post, doing his duty. During the latter part of the battle, a captain, an intimate friend, fell, severely wounded. He caught him in his arms, and laid him gently on the ground, pillowing his head in his lap. The regiment moved off, and the rebels advanced; but he refused to leave his friend. And he did not leave until the captain was borne away by his comrades. He passed through this battle without a scratch. He accompanied the regiment to Alexandria, and from there to the front of Pope's army. He now took part in the battle of Cedar Mountain. While cheering his men forward, he was wounded. Two men took him in their arms, and started in search of the hospital; but before they were off the field a bullet struck him in the groin, severing the femoral artery. Said he, "Remember, boys, I die for my country," and expired in their arms. Thus, a true and devoted friend of his country died to preserve it from the attacks of those who had been educated and supported by it from boyhood.

As an officer, Lieutenant Brisbine was much esteemed; as a companion, he was admired by every one. I doubt if he had an enemy in the army or at home. He won his promotion in the field; and it was, therefore, a much greater prize than a higher rank conferred by favor. He was commissioned early in 1862.

LIEUTENANT CHARLES A. BROOKS.

The subject of this sketch was born in Bristol, Trumbull County, in the year 1843. He early developed those good qualities of head and heart for which he was afterwards so distinguished. Being a good student, attentive to his books, as he was to every other good purpose, he acquired a good education, which would have enabled him to engage in any occupation with credit to himself and profit to the community.

He was desirous of entering the service when the war first began, but was held back by domestic ties which bound him strongly to home. But on the second call for troops, he could no longer remain out of the army; and, hastening to a recruiting station, he enlisted in Company H, of the Seventh Regiment. He arrived at Camp Dennison on the 30th of May, and, with others, was mustered into the service. His tall, commanding figure, connected with his sterling qualities of mind, pointed him out as a proper person for promotion. He was, therefore made a corporal, and, as soon as a vacancy occurred, a sergeant. His officers soon put unlimited confidence in him. If a hazardous enterprise was to be performed, he was deemed fitting to undertake it. While still a sergeant, Creighton would often point him out as his future adjutant. Finally, when Adjutant Shepherd was compelled to resign, on account of growing ill health, Creighton procured his appointment as first-lieutenant, and at once detailed him as his adjutant. He came to this position entirely qualified; for, from the time he had been made orderly of Company H, he transacted all of the business of the company. He was in the affair at Cross Lanes, and all other skirmishes in which the regiment was engaged, as well as the following battles: Port Republic, Cedar Mountain, Dumfries, Chancellorsville, and Gettysburg.

Near the close of the battle of Port Republic, he saw one of his old officers lying, seriously wounded, so near the enemy's lines as to be in danger of capture. Throwing down his gun, in company with Charles Garrard, he braved the battle-fire, and brought his old comrade safely from the field; thus, probably, saving his life.

At the battle of Cedar Mountain he was slightly wounded, losing a finger.

In July he was sent to Ohio to bring forward the drafted men assigned to the Seventh. While on his way from Columbus to his home in Bristol, he met with a frightful accident resulting in death. While seated in an omnibus, it was driven on to the railroad track, directly in front of a train. In jumping out, he was knocked down by the cars and run over, mangling both legs frightfully. He was taken to the New England House, but nothing could be done for him, and he expired early the following morning. The following is from the pen of one who knew him and prized him:[6]

"The career of this young man has been short but brilliant. He has been a soldier and a man; pure, noble-hearted, sympathetic, and always ready for any duty. He has been brave, courageous, and trustworthy. He has gone from us with no stain upon his honor, no spots upon his escutcheon, but with his armor begrimed with the dust of many battles. Although young in years, he had lived long, if you count the hardships he had endured, the stirring and momentous events through which he had passed, and in the transpiring of which he had been an actor, the service he rendered his country, and humanity at large, and the good he had done; if gauged by this standard, he had become more mature than many men who have attained their threescore and ten years. So bright an example cannot fail to have a good influence upon the young men of the country. His violent death will bring his virtues prominently before their minds, and cannot fail to make an impression. Let all be exhorted to emulate his patriotism, his gallantry, his valor, his promptness in the discharge of duty, his kindness of heart, suavity of manner, his manly and soldier-like qualities; and if in civil life, they will become manlier men—if in military life, they cannot fail to become better and braver soldiers."

He was buried near where he was born, on the banks of a rippling brook, under the shade of beautiful trees, through the boughs of which will sing an everlasting requiem fitting so brave and active a spirit. The citizens of the vicinity turned out in mass to honor his memory with their presence, and tearful eyes and expressive looks showed their heartfelt sympathy for the afflicted mother, sister, brother, and relatives; while a military organization from Warren gave him the fitting escort, and fired three volleys over his grave.

A grateful public will not forget this heroic and noble sacrifice. Let an enduring monument be erected. Not of marble, which may crumble; but let his manly deeds be engraved upon the tablets of their memory, and let his virtues and sacrifices be interwoven with the affections, the sympathies, and the lives of the people, so that while time lasts, and all that is noble in human action, good in thought, and true in conception and motive, shall be treasured as sacred memories, this hero will not be forgotten, because kept fresh with the watering of many tears.

LIEUTENANT JOSEPH H. ROSS.

Joseph H. Ross entered the service as a private in Captain W. R. Sterling's company. Soon after arriving in camp he was made a sergeant, and finally orderly.

He was engaged in all the marches and skirmishes in Western Virginia, and at Cross Lanes fought like a veteran. He was in the battle of Winchester, where he displayed such reckless bravery as to attract the attention of the entire command. While the regiment was partially concealed behind a ridge, within eighty yards of the enemy, Ross was not content with remaining at such a distance, but creeping over the hill, crawled forward on his hands and knees till he was midway between the lines, and taking a position behind a rock, swung his hat to those behind. None but Sergeant Whiting, of Company D, had the courage to follow him. From behind this rock, the two heroes kept up a constant fire on the enemy, hitting their man at every shot.

Ross was now made a lieutenant, and assigned to Company C. He was in the battle of Port Republic, where he fought with his usual bravery. At the battle of Cedar Mountain he commanded Company C. During the entire day he led his men with such certainty, that they slaughtered the enemy fearfully. Night came, and he had not received a scratch, while the thinned ranks testified how many had fallen around him. Soon after dark, as if the regiment had not already suffered sufficiently, it was ordered on picket. When about a mile out, it was fired upon from all quarters, and Lieutenant Ross fell, mortally wounded. He died soon after. His loss was deeply felt, both in the army and at home; for he was a true soldier and friend.

LIEUTENANT FRANK JOHNSON.

At this same bloody battle of Cedar Mountain, another youthful hero fell, Frank Johnson, Company F. He had entered the service as a private in John Man's company, and had risen through the different grades of corporal and sergeant to be a lieutenant. He had toiled along through the hard marches of the Seventh, struggling against a weak constitution, which was every day being impaired by hardships and exposure. He had fought nobly in the battles of Winchester and Port Republic,—recognized by the authorities by giving him a commission; and now, in the morning of his new life as a *leader*, he fell at the head of his company.

Footnotes

[1]
Charles Tenney.

[2]
Lieutenant W. D. Shepherd.

[3]
General Tyler has failed to furnish us any data from which to write an extended sketch, though often requested to do so.

[4]
The writer has been unable to learn sufficient of General Sprague's services, after leaving the Seventh, to enable him to write an extended sketch, which he very much regrets, for his gallant services entitle him to a more lengthy notice.

[5]
The writer would be glad to give an extended account of the gallant services of

Colonel Shurtliff in the bloody battles before Richmond and Petersburg, but has not received the necessary facts.

[6]

Colonel J. F. Asper.